Woman, Why Weepest Thou?
Mary Magdalene: Liberated by Love

A Christian Character Study

Jason Derome Moore

Woman, Why Weepest Thou?
Mary Magdalene: Liberated by Love
Copyright © 2009

A Christian Character Study
by Jason Derome Moore

Unless otherwise designated, all Scriptures are taken from the Holy Bible, the New King James Version® (NKJV). Copyright © 1982 by Thomas Nelson. Used by permission. All rights reserved.

All Scriptures designated (KJV) are taken from the Holy Bible, the King James Version, Public Domain.

All Scriptures designated (MSG) are taken from the Holy Bible, The Message (MSG) Copyright © 1993, 1994, 1995, 1996, 2000, 2001, 2002 by Eugene H. Peterson.

For copies of this book, contact:
Jason Moore
PO Box 261
Rockwall, Texas 75087
jmoore@ontherockchurch.org

DEDICATION

Personally to my girls: Lakisha, Patricia, and Linda.

Publicly to every man who has a past he's not proud of; to every woman who has been beaten, battered, and bruised at the hands of a man or by the hands of time and trials and everyone who has experienced his or her share of letdowns and disappointments.

May I assure you all that *"Those who sow in tears shall reap in joy, and he who continually goes forth weeping, bearing seed for sowing, shall doubtless come again with rejoicing, bringing his sheaves with him"* (Psalm 126:5, 6).

ACKNOWLEDGMENTS

MANY HAVE WORKED hard alongside of me to bring this book into fruition. Largely because of you, what once was only a distant dream is now reality. Words cannot express my gratitude. Thank you! Among the many are four whom I must acknowledge specifically and publicly:

Joseph Paden, thank you for all of your energy and effort that you put into this project. It will not be forgotten by God or me.

Aldower Jones, you saw what I couldn't see. You started the ball rolling and believed in me when I did not believe in myself. Thank you!

Todd Vincent, your friendship throughout this short period of time has proven to be genuine, tried and true. Along with your friendship has come your sacrifice and service on a work that became much better because of your zeal and skill. Thanks, brother! The following Scripture applies to all of you:

"For God is not unjust to forget your work and labor of love which you have shown towards His name, in that you have ministered to the saints, and do minister" (Hebrews 6:10).

Last, but certainly not least, apart from the Lord Jesus Christ, none of this would have been possible. Apart from

Him, I am nothing! Apart from Him, I can do nothing! Therefore any glory that this book brings about goes to my Master and Messiah, Jesus the Christ. *"He who glories, let him glory in the Lord"* (1 Corinthians 1:31).

TABLE OF CONTENTS

Preface 9

Part One: Her Demons
Chapter One
    Baggage and Bondage 13

Part Two: Her Deliverance
Chapter Two
    Operation Liberation............................. 25

Part Three: Her Devotion
Chapter Three
    A Faithful Follower 41
Chapter Four
    Sold Out or Sell Out?............................ 51
Chapter Five
    What's Love Got to Do With It?................... 65

Part Four: Her Disappointment
Chapter Six
    The Worse Weekend Ever........................ 81

Woman, Why Weepest Thou?

PART FIVE: HER DAYLIGHT

Chapter Seven
    When Midnight Turns to Daylight 95

PART SIX: OUR DEPOSIT

Epilogue
    A Message in a Bottle 111

Scripture Index 117
Benediction 123

PREFACE

THE BIBLE IS FULL of prominent and prudent women of faith, virtue, courage, and character, women of outer and inner beauty. So when it came time for me to choose just one about whom to write, I was like a kid in a candy store. Yet after much prayer and meditation the choice was crystal-clear: *Mary Magdalene.*

No woman in scripture has endured as much verbal victimization and controversial chatter as Mary Magdalene. Her character has been assassinated and attacked, mislabeled, and misunderstood throughout the years by both Christians and critics alike. Some of this misunderstanding is out of ignorance of the Holy Scriptures and some out of irreverence for them.

All this misunderstanding led me on a search to find out exactly who this Mary was and who she wasn't. You are holding in your hands the results of my personal research. The birth of this book comes from an intense Biblical investigation into the life of Mary Magdalene from the pages of Scripture. What I discovered not only confronted and convicted me, it also challenged and changed me. Hopefully, the results of your reading will be somewhat similar.

As your life encounters Mary's life, my earnest prayer is that

Woman, Why Weepest Thou?

you will leave knowing what I left knowing, and that is, there's a little bit of Mary Magdalene in all of us. The same Savior who loved her loves you. Most of all, I pray that you'll leave knowing that if a woman with a checkered past such as hers can deeply love Jesus and remain loyal to Him until the end, so can you!

– Jason D. Moore

Part One
Her Demons

"There are two equal opposite errors into which our race can fall about devils. One is disbelief in their existence. The other is to believe and to feel unhealthy interest in them. They themselves are pleased by both."

– C. S. LEWIS

CHAPTER ONE

BAGGAGE AND BONDAGE

"And certain women, which had been healed of evil spirits and infirmities, Mary called Magdalene, out of whom went seven devils" (Luke 8:2, KJV).

D<small>O YOU BELIEVE</small> in demons? Do you believe in the Devil? Below is an excerpt from a letter I received December 15, 2007. The writer of the letter has granted me permission to share the following excerpts. To protect her privacy, I will keep her name anonymous. I only ask that you read what she shared with an open mind and heart.

A Convincing Letter
That Demands Consideration

Jason, I'm not sure about anything right now. I'm not sure about us, the future, or anything. When all this stuff started happening between us, I didn't understand what was really going on. But now I know it was God bringing everything to the light. Before everything came out, I had begun to ask the Lord to make me more like Him. I told

Woman, Why Weepest Thou?

Him that if there were things in me that were not like Him, to expose it and clean me out. That whole situation came about because I asked the Lord to clean me out. Ever since then, that's what the Lord has being doing.

Much like you, before all of this took place, I didn't believe that Christians could have demons. However, after much examination of the Scriptures, and my own recent experiences, I have come to believe very differently. The truth of the matter is there was a time that none of us lived for God. We were all out there doing our own thing. While we were doing our own thing, we were opening doors to Satan and his demons to come in.

Then, there came a time in our lives when we met Jesus. We invited Him in, and our lives got better. However, we reached a point where we couldn't go any farther. No matter how much we prayed, read the Bible, went to church, etc., something was still hindering our growth. As it turns out, in our past we opened doors to the spiritual realm of evil and darkness and never dealt with it. We invited in some things because of family members and curses. No matter how they got there the fact remains that they are there and they need to be cast out! I agree that some things are strongholds in the mind that need to be pulled down. However, there are other things that are inside deep within those hidden places of the heart. Once the Lord begins exposing those things, we realize how ugly we are. Yes, if we belong to God, it can't stay there. That's why deliverance must take place.

People can say whatever they want about deliverance. The truth of the matter is I know what's there. I know how I feel when they're there. It's a constant battle.

The Reality of Demonic Possession and Oppression

As you can see, the letter you have read was a very personal and serious letter. I decided to share such a private letter with you for one main purpose: to assure you that demonic oppression and demonic possession are not a figment of any person's capricious imagination. They are real, and the experience was real for the young lady who wrote me that letter.

Likewise, the oppression and possession were real for the case study in this book: Mary Magdalene. If anyone could attest to the fact that demons are real, Mary Magdalene could. If anyone could attest to the fact that demons have power to both influence and indwell a person, Mary could.

Satan and His Fall

What exactly are demons? Where did they originate? It all goes back to Satan and his fall from heaven. According to Isaiah 14:12-14, Ezekiel 28:12-17 and 1 Timothy 3:6, Satan fell because of pride. Jesus Himself declared in Luke 10:18 that He saw "Satan fall like lighting from heaven." All this is worth mentioning because in Satan's fall from heaven, he took down some more angels with him—one third of the angels, to be exact (Revelation 12:4). When Satan fell, they fell right alongside of him. These angels are now referred to as *fallen angels*, de-

mons, or *devils* as Luke describes them in reference to Mary Magdalene.

Satan's Name and Game

Satan's name provides great insight into his character. The name *Satan* means "adversary." Another familiar name for Satan also gives great insight into his character—*Devil,* which means "accuser." Combining both names—Satan and Devil—gives an accurate description of this evil angelic being and his task. He is the one who daily accuses the child of God and is constantly and continually opposing the work and will of God.

Mary's Possession

Mary Magdalene was no stranger to Satan. She was no stranger to the Strongman and his power to erect a stronghold in one's life. She knew all too well how it felt to be a slave to Satan and his minions.

Two gospel writers, Mark and Luke, mention a time when Mary Magdalene was possessed by seven demons. At that time, her life was full of baggage and bondage. Mary Magdalene was at one time demonically possessed.

Possession Vs. Oppression

The difference between demon possession and demon oppression is worth explaining. Naturally, if a person is not a Christian, he can be demon-possessed. That person's whole body and being can belong to the Devil and his demons. Obviously, the levels of demon-possession are different, but every non-believer is demonically possessed to some degree or another.

However, if a person is a Christian, he cannot be demon-possessed, but he can be demon-oppressed, which means demons can oppress his mind, will, and emotions (soul). It also means demons can oppress the person's body. Even though demon possession and demon oppression look a lot alike from the perspective of the observer, there's a huge difference. Possession indicates ownership, while oppression indicates harsh and cruel tyrannical treatment.

By no means am I saying Christians cannot have demons, but what I am saying is demons can never *own* a Christian. Control? Yes! Influence? Yes! Harass and disturb? Yes! But own? No! Therefore, the issue is an issue of possession versus oppression. In other words, possession is an issue of ownership.

As Christians, we belong to God. As Christians, we've been bought with a price. As Christians, we've been purchased with the precious blood of the Lamb. Paul the apostle once wrote, "*...do you not know that your body is the temple of the Holy Spirit who is in you, whom you have from God, and you are not your own? For you were bought at a price...*" (1 Corinthians 6:19, 20, NKJV). As Christians, our ownership belongs to God. In fact, He's the owner of every Christian. Therefore, a Christian can never be owned or possessed by the Devil and his demons.

That ownership, though, is not true for the unbeliever and certainly was not true in the case of Mary Magdalene. The truth is that there was a time in Mary Magdalene's life when she did not belong to God; she belonged to Satan and his demons. During this time, Mary Magdalene was in bondage to seven demons, and her life was full of baggage. What you might not know is Mary Magdalene's baggage and bondage is directly linked to her background.

Demonic Doorways and Gateways

For demons to possess, oppress, indwell, or influence anyone, a door must be opened. Permission or consent has to be given. A gateway must be granted. Contrary to what many have been taught, demons do not impose themselves on anyone; they only come in by invitation. A common doorway is behavior. A person who is constantly disobeying God can expect to have problems with demons. Another doorway for demons to come in is through a person's background. This doorway has to do with our past and the place in which we were reared. This doorway is the one on which I want to concentrate in the case of Mary Magdalene.

Mary's Background

What exactly was Mary Magdalene's background? Where was she reared? What was her past? Her name alone provides some insight into her life. *Mary Magdalene* literally means "Mary of Magdala." Magdala was a small fishing village located on the northwestern shore of the Sea of Galilee, north of the Roman city of Tiberius, about five and a half miles south and west from Capernaum. Jesus performed many exorcisms in this area, which means Mary Magdalene's hometown and the surrounding region must have been a common spot for spiritual wickedness and warfare.

Considering the area where Mary Magdalene was reared helps to gain understanding of why she was in the shape she was. Her surroundings and scenery played a vital role in her becoming ensnared and enslaved to evil. She was around evil daily. The chances are that some of Mary Magdalene's family members and childhood friends were caught up in this ever-present evil. Certainly, if this supposition is true, the chances of Mary Magdalene's becoming a victim to such an evil environment would have been enhanced. A person can only rub elbows with evil for so long before he or she becomes overtaken. Evil eventually rubbed off on Mary Magdalene. In fact, evil didn't simply get *on* her; it got *in* her—not one time, not two or three times, but *seven* times.

Mary's Bondage

The number *seven* in the Bible signifies "completion," which would mean that Mary Magdalene's bondage to the forces of darkness was complete. Hers was a done deal, not a partial possession. Satan had her tied up, tangled up, and locked up in his prison forever, or so he thought.

Think about Mary Magdalene's bondage. This woman was not possessed by one demon; she was possessed by seven. In the New Testament, some of the symptoms of demonic possession include insanity and suicidal tendencies (Mark 5:1-5), blindness and dumbness (Matthew 12:22), deafness (Mark 9:17-27), seizures (Matthew 17:15), and chronic ailment (Luke 13:11-13).

These symptoms alone provide a glimpse and a little insight on how difficult life must have been for Mary Magdalene. Satan tormented her constantly and continually. Not a day went by where she didn't feel his presence and his demons breathing down her neck.

Mary's Baggage

In his book *Twelve Extraordinary Women: How the Master Shaped His Disciples for Greatness, and What He Wants to Do with You,* Pastor John F. MacArthur captures what I am trying to relay concerning Mary Magdalene more candidly:

> *There was nothing* any mere man or woman could do for her. She was a veritable prisoner of demonic afflictions. These undoubtedly included depression, anxiety, unhappiness, loneliness, self-loathing, shame, fear, and a host of other similar miseries. In all probability, she suffered even worse torments too, such as blindness, deafness, insanity, or any of the other disorders commonly associated with victims of demonic possession described in the New Testament. Whatever her condition, she would have been in perpetual agony, at least seven kinds of agony.[1]

Dr. MacArthur's description of Mary Magdalene helps tremendously in portraying how terrible life was for her. Still, I am inclined to believe no matter how the effects of her demonic possession are described, we cannot come close to truly comprehending how much this woman truly suffered. It's greater

Baggage and Bondage

than we could ever imagine. Her background, her bondage, her torment and her torture encompass far more than our finite minds could ever grasp. All that she endured is much worse than any of us could ever imagine.

Mary in Me? Me in Mary?

I want to address one more fact about Mary Magdalene that I wish to bring to your attention in this chapter. I discovered that nothing is mentioned in the Gospels about Mary Magdalene's age, outward appearance or marital status.

Seemingly, these descriptions and other similar ones were left unsaid intentionally. God, the ultimate Author of Scripture, left these characteristics about Mary Magdalene open to our spiritual imagination. The fact is leaving them open to our spiritual imagination allows us to see Mary Magdalene from a variety of angles. Mary could have been any height, any weight, married, single, or divorced. Simply put, Mary Magdalene could have been any one of us.

If you see some of Mary Magdalene in you, please continue to the next chapter. Bondage, baggage, and a bad background did not have the final say in Mary Magdalene's life, and neither do these conditions have to have the final say in your life either. There is hope. You can be delivered from darkness and every demon.

A Prayer to Pray

Father in Heaven, before going any further in this book and turning another page, we pause and let what we just read really register and sink in. The truth is at this very hour in time some of us are in bondage and loaded down with baggage just like Mary. Some of us are at this place in life because of demonic possession; others of us are at this place in life because of demonic oppression. And even though the cause may differ the results are the same. We are addicted. We are caught up. We are ensnared. We are enslaved. And we desperately need deliverance.

Lord, our actions throughout this time in our lives have left us not only ashamed but afraid. Yet we know and believe that there is still hope. So look deep within our heart and do a spiritual surgery that will enable us to walk freely and victoriously. Liberate and emancipate us by the power of Your Holy Spirit through Your only begotten Son, Jesus Christ. Take the scales off our eyes and the shackles off our minds. Set us free! For those whom the Son sets free are free indeed. In His name I pray this prayer. Amen.

---

[1]John MacArthur, *Twelve Extraordinary Women: How the Master Shaped His Disciples for Greatness, and What He Wants to Do with You* (Nashville: Thomas Nelson, 2006), 175.

Part Two
Her Deliverance

"Millions of angels are at God's command and at our service. The host of heaven stands at attention as we make our way from earth to glory, and Satan's BB guns are no match for God's heavy artillery."

– BILLY GRAHAM

CHAPTER TWO

OPERATION LIBERATION

"...he [Jesus] appeared first to Mary Magdalene, out of whom he had cast seven devils" (Mark 16:9, KJV).

A Perfect Operation

THROUGHOUT THE YEARS, the Pentagon and each military branch have launched many operations. Some of these operations have been more than successful while others have seemingly fallen short in accomplishing their original goal and purpose. This failure should come as no surprise though, because imperfect people can never produce a perfect operation that does not leave behind a few casualties or lose a few battles along the way.

There is One, however, who is perfect. His operation can also be described as perfect in the sense that it never failed and in the sense that it accomplished exactly what it was ordained and originated to accomplish. That perfect One is Jesus, and He, even at the age of twelve, had this operation on His mind. How He once responded to His parents' inquiry is found in Luke 2:49, which says, *And He said to them, "Why did you seek Me? Did you not know that I must be about My Father's business?"*

At an early age, Jesus had His mind on His operation and His operation on His mind.

The Meaning of *Operation*

When I refer to the word *operation* throughout this chapter, I have in mind "a divine task or assignment or a God-ordained duty that a person is sent forth to perform."

The questions that must now be answered include the following:
- What was Jesus' operation?
- What was His divine task or assignment?
- What was His God-ordained duty?

If you will permit me to do so, I prefer to let the Word of God answer those questions.

Jesus and His Operation

The writer Luke records a scene in chapter four of his gospel that beautifully answers those questions. Jesus was revisiting His former hometown of Nazareth. While there, He attended a worship service in the synagogue on the Sabbath day. During the worship service, He stood up and began to read from Isaiah 61:1, 2 (KJV), which says:

> "The Spirit of the Lord GOD is upon me; because the LORD hath anointed me to preach good tidings unto the meek; he hath sent me to bind up the brokenhearted, to proclaim liberty to the captives, and the opening of the prison to them that are bound; To proclaim the acceptable year of the LORD...."

Operation Liberation

Jesus' operation was to preach the gospel to the poor, heal the brokenhearted, preach deliverance to the captives, restore sight to the blind, to set at liberty those who were bruised, and to preach the acceptable year of the Lord. These specific duties described in detail what Jesus' operation consisted of. They were the *core* of His operation, in other words. And notice, the Spirit of the Lord had anointed Him to perform these divine task. The Spirit of the Lord had empowered Him and enabled Him to accomplish this God-given assignment.

The Operation and the Validation

After quoting those verses from Isaiah 61:1 and 2, Jesus said in Luke 4:21 (KJV), *"This day is this scripture fulfilled in your ears."* The hearers doubted what Jesus was claiming and made the comment, *"is not this Joseph's son?"* (v. 22, KJV). What Jesus was claiming by quoting those verses was clear as a bell to all, especially when He followed it up by saying that fulfillment of that Scripture was taking place right then and there. Without any doubt, Jesus was making an unambiguous claim that He was the promised Messiah who was fulfilling the prophecy of the prophet Isaiah. In other words, Jesus' operation served as validation of His being the Messiah.

Not long after this episode in Nazareth, John the Baptist, the forerunner of Jesus, was imprisoned. While John was in prison, he sent two of his disciples to ask Jesus a question. The question was, "Are You the coming one, or do we look for another?" (Matthew 11:3). John was asking Jesus in no uncertain terms, "Are you the Messiah, or do we look for another?"

Jesus answered John's question in a very profound manner. Read His answer carefully.

> *"Jesus answered and said to them, go and tell John the things which you hear and see: The blind see, and the lame walk; the lepers are cleansed and the deaf hear; the dead are raised up and the poor have the Gospel preached to them"* (Matthew 11:4, 5).

John asked the question in no uncertain terms, and Jesus answered in no uncertain terms. In His answer, Jesus quoted from two Messianic promises: Isaiah 35:5, 6 and Isaiah 61:1. By quoting these verses, Jesus was saying to John, "Yes, I am the Messiah. My proof? I am doing precisely what the Scriptures foretold of the Messiah. I'm healing the blind, the deaf, and the lame. I'm cleansing lepers, raising the dead, and preaching the gospel to the poor."

John's disciples were to deliver this report to John. They were to tell him about the things they had heard and had seen Jesus perform. And John would be able to "connect the dots" and see that what Jesus was doing lined up with what Scripture prophesied about the coming Messiah.

Therefore, every time Jesus preached, He proved He was the Messiah. Every instance of healing a broken heart proved that He was the Messiah. Every time He raised the dead proved that He was the Messiah. Every time He gave sight to the blind proved that He was the Messiah. Every time He gave hearing to the deaf proved that He was the Messiah. Every time He caused the lame to walk and the mute to talk proved that He was the

Messiah. Jesus' operation was validation of His being the Messiah. His fulfilling of the divine assignment of preaching and healing proved the authenticity of His being the Messiah.

Being the promised Messiah simply meant that Jesus had come to liberate some folks, deliver some folks, and heal some folks. Jesus' operation was essentially an operation of liberation. He came to liberate those who were in slavery to Satan and sin. He came to break their bondage and to heal their hurt. He came to reverse the curse. Simply put, Jesus came to set the captives free!

The Meeting of Mary and the Messiah

Surely, Mary Magdalene, the central character of this book, falls into the category of a *captive*. That thought was established in the preceding chapter when Mary Magdalene was enslaved to seven demons. She was held captive mentally, physically, emotionally and spiritually. At one time, before she met Jesus and before she was rescued through "Operation Liberation," her life was shackled and in shambles.

Remember, Mary Magdalene's having seven demons signified that she was in complete bondage. Her having seven demons signified that her bondage and possession were complete, the deal was sealed, and she was to be a prisoner of the Devil and his demons forever.

But the truth is, Jesus has the power to overturn and override any sentence from Satan, and that deliverance is exactly what took place in Mary Magdalene's life. She was supposed to be in Satan's prison of darkness and depravity forever, but Jesus overturned and overrode that sentence. That liberty Mary

Magdalene experienced proves firmly that it doesn't matter how far or how low Satan has taken a person. It does not matter how long he has held a person captive. If Jesus commands, "Loose that man and let him go," or "Loose that woman and let her go," Satan has no choice but to comply. Never forget that God's power always trumps Satan's power! Satan thought he had Mary Magdalene forever, but he thought wrong! Through a chain of unmentioned events in the Scriptures, Mary Magdalene somehow met the Messiah, and when she met Him, her life was forever changed.

Set Up to Be Set Free

Perhaps before Mary Magdalene met Jesus, she was poor in spirit, and He preached the gospel to her for He had been anointed to preach the gospel to the poor. Before she met Him, perhaps she was brokenhearted, and He healed her broken heart for He had been sent to heal the brokenhearted. Before she met Him, perhaps she was bruised, and He liberated her for He had come to set at liberty those who had been bruised.

Before she met Him, we do know she was spiritually blind and a captive to Satan and sin, but Jesus brought into her life recovery of sight and deliverance from captivity because He had been sent to preach deliverance to the captives and recovery of sight to the blind. Jesus set Mary Magdalene free. Consider the words that Jesus said of Himself in John 8:36: *"Therefore if the Son makes you free, you shall be free indeed."*

When Mary Magdalene met the Messiah, she became free indeed. Mark's gospel account refers to her as "...*Mary Mag-*

dalene, out of whom He [Jesus] had cast seven demons" (Mark 16:9). Luke's gospel account refers to her as "Mary called Magdalene, out of whom had come seven demons" (Luke 8:2). Both gospel writers seem to imply that Mary Magdalene's deliverance was instant, complete, and total. That's amazing because Mary Magdalene's days of walking in darkness were supposedly complete and final. However, when Jesus showed up on the scene of Mary's life, He proved otherwise. He proved that Mary Magdalene's darkness wasn't complete or final, but her deliverance would be!

On that day Jesus proved something to Mary and to others that should be remembered. The Savior has the last say—not Satan! Nothing is final or forever unless it's uttered from the lips of the Lord. Satan may have the audacity to call a situation complete, final, or forever, but he does not have the authority to do it. Only Jesus does!

Because of Jesus, Mary Magdalene was no longer Mary Magdalene who *"has"* seven demons. She was now Mary Magdalene who once *"had"* seven demons. Before she met Jesus, she had seven demons and seven demons had her. In the present, neither of the two was true. She had been set free—eternally emancipated through her divine encounter with Jesus Christ, the CEO of "Operation Liberation." She had been set up to be set free!

Personal and Practical Application

Now it's time for a little up-close, personal, and practical application: Jesus can also set *you* free. The amount of baggage you carry does not matter. How atrocious your background may be does not matter. The awful effects of your bondage do not matter. You haven't sunk so low or went so far that Jesus cannot reach out with His encircling arms of love and liberate you. He has never met His match, and I seriously doubt you'll be the first. Trust me; you're no match for Him. Jesus has both the power and passion to deliver you from anything and everything that is holding you hostage. He can set you free! He longs to do for you what He did for Mary Magdalene. He longs to liberate you. The question is: "Will you let Him?"

Love Without a Limit

Before proceeding to the next chapter, another lingering question of *why* needs to be addressed. Why did Jesus liberate Mary Magdalene? Was it because of her good looks or good lifestyle? Was it something she did or did not do? Was it something she said or did not say? Was it because she was such an outstanding citizen in the community? Was it because she had dotted all her *i*'s and crossed all her *t*'s? Was it because she already had everything together? I seriously doubt it.

The reason why Jesus liberated Mary Magdalene is found in one word: love. His unconditional and unchanging love for her caused Him to liberate her. His outpouring of love is plain and profound at the same time. Christ couldn't stand to see Mary Magdalene in her distress any longer. He loved her too much—not with a polluted or perverted love as some so-called scholars have tried to suggest—but with a pure and perfect love. His pure love refused to let her keep on living the way she had been living. Jesus loved her, and guess what? He loves you too! He loves you with no strings attached. He does not love you so He can take advantage of you. He simply loves you for who you are—exactly as you are. I have the feeling that perhaps you needed to read of His love.

Maybe you have been waiting for an estranged spouse to say, "I love you." Maybe you've been waiting for a rebellious or wayward child to say, "I love you." Maybe you've been waiting for a parent, a distant family member, or even a friend to say, "I love you," but that declaration of love has yet to happen. The truth is, the person you need to hear declare his or her love may never do so. You may never hear what you desperately long to hear. So, my friend, hear it from Jesus today. Hear Jesus say, "I love you."

Hear Jesus say, "Though I know the depths of your heart, though I know every detail of your life, though I know the sins of your past, present, and future, I still love you."

How much does Jesus really love you? Your answer is found in John 15:13, which says, *"Greater love has no one than this, than to lay down one's life for his friends."*

That verse says how much Jesus loves you. He loves you so much that He laid down His life for you. He loves you so much that He chose to go to Calvary and suffer for you, rather than to go to heaven without you. His love exemplifies real love. Let that thought liberate you!

Love Lifted Me

When I came to this point in writing this book, I found it difficult not to think about my own life before conversion. Talk about darkness and depravity to the umpteenth degree. For twenty-two years, I was in bondage to the Devil and demons galore.

Sin, Satan, and self had taken me faster and farther than I had wanted to go, had kept me longer than I wanted to stay, and had cost me more than I was able to pay. Except for a few family members and friends, everyone had thrown in the towel on me. Basically, they all had given up on me. As far as they were concerned, my life was ruined and over forever. My ruin was seemingly final.

The deal seemed to have been sealed, and I would remain forever in my sinful state, but God, who is rich in grace and mercy, reached down and reached out in love and brought me out of the darkness into the marvelous light. I was immediately and instantly emancipated and exonerated through my divine encounter with Jesus. His love lifted me. His love liberated me.

My friend, isn't it about time you let His love do the same for you? What are you waiting for?

Point to Ponder

A point worthy of pondering before turning another page has to do with cleaning up your life versus cleaning out your life. Here's the point: you have the power to *clean up* your life, but you do not possess the power to *clean out* your life. Only Jesus does! Follow me thoughtfully as I put this thought in another way. A life that is reformed apart from repentance and regeneration is a life that will eventually revert to past behaviors or even worse.

In Matthew 12:43-45, Jesus tells a story that illustrates this point in a very powerful way.

> *"When an unclean spirit goes out of a man, he goes through dry places, seeking rest, and finds none. Then he says, 'I will return to my house from which I came.' And when he comes, he finds it empty, swept, and put in order. Then he goes and takes with him seven other spirits more wicked than himself, and they enter and dwell there; and the last state of that man is worse than the first...."*

Two profound truths have always stood out to me from this passage. First, the spirit referred to the person as "my house"—and he wasn't referring to a physical house constructed of wood or brick. Secondly, when the spirit came back to check out "his house," he found it empty. Both truths point toward the futility of self-reform, which eventually only makes matters worse.

The man in the story is a clear example of someone who has cleaned *up* his life, but he hasn't allowed Christ to clean *out* his life. If Christ had done the renovation, the house would no longer have been empty nor would it have belonged to the evil spirit. On the contrary, the house would have belonged to Christ and would have been full through the indwelling presence of the Holy Spirit as opposed to empty.

The man in the story paints a vivid picture of a person who spends a lifetime cleaning up the *fruit* of his sin, but he never allows Jesus to come in and clean out the root of his sin. Exterior changes such as sweeping the house and putting rooms and belongings in order are both insufficient and inadequate; they can never release the person from the domination of darkness and Satan's gruesome grip. Only Jesus can!

Much like the man in Jesus' story is the man who is sentenced to prison. While in prison, he is separated from what has contributed to his downfall, so he begins to clean up his life. Though his change comes mainly by force rather than choice, he stops drinking and getting drunk. He stops committing adultery and fornicating. He stops robbing, stealing, and killing. He stops selling drugs and using drugs. He cleans up all his exterior actions and habits. But soon as he gets out, he often returns to those same old habits and behaviors and even worse. Why? Because he cleaned up his life, but he never allowed Jesus to come in and clean out his life. Remember the point to ponder? You have the power to clean up your life, but you do not possess the power to clean out your life. Only Jesus does!

Centuries before Jesus ever told His illustrative story, the prophet Jeremiah spoke the same truth in fewer words. He said:

> *"Can the Ethiopian change his skin or the leopard its spots? Then may you also do good who are accustomed to do evil"* (Jeremiah 13:23).

Just like the Ethiopian can't change his skin color or the leopard its spots, neither can a person change his life. Only Jesus can! Mankind was born depraved, incurably sick with sin, and Christ alone has the cure. The sooner mankind realizes this fact, the better off he will be. Yes, you may be able to clean up your life, but only Christ can clean out your life. For Christ to clean out your life, you must come to the end of your rope. You must come to the end of yourself and your strength. You must humbly admit that your life is full of dirt and darkness, and you do not have the strength or power to clean it out; only Jesus does!

Please ponder that point. Somewhere along the way, Mary Magdalene came to this point in her life, and my friend, you must get there too. Today is a good day to get there. Are you there yet?

Part Three
Her Devotion

"All I have seen teaches me to trust the Creator for all I have not seen."

– RALPH WALDO EMERSON

CHAPTER THREE

A FAITHFUL FOLLOWER

"And certain women, which had been healed of evil spirits and infirmities, Mary called Magdalene, out of whom went seven devils. And Joanna the wife of Chuza Herod's steward, and Susanna, and many others, which ministered unto him of their substance" (Luke 8:2, KJV).

Loopholes and Loyalty

FINDING LOYALTY NOWADAYS is comparable to trying to find a needle in a haystack; the task is very difficult. Loyalty is a missing trait that desperately needs rediscovering. Long gone are the days when a person could be trusted to uphold a commitment without having to sign some type of written contract or agreement. These days most people seem to be looking for a loophole when it comes to the trait of loyalty. People seem to be seeking a reason to go rather than a reason to stay, a way out rather than a way through.

An Exception on the Verge of Extinction

But not Mary Magdalene. If she was anything, she was loyal and faithful to the core. She was a true, authentic woman of integrity and virtue. For the record, those types of men and women are hard to find. Proverbs 20:6 asks a revealing question that shows the rarity of a faithful or loyal man: *"...who can find a faithful man?"* Proverbs 31:10 also asks a similar question: *"Who can find a virtuous wife?"* (NKJV). The apparent implication of both verses is that faithful men and women are rare and difficult to find. Therefore, Mary Magdalene was a rare exception—one on the verge of extinction, I might add. But how could Mary Magdalene not be loyal? After all, you must remember the shape she was in before she met her Messiah and Master. She had once had seven demons telling her what to say, what to do, and where to go. Jesus took away all that dissonance in her life and wiped her slate clean. For such an enormous gift, Mary Magdalene had to be grateful, and gratefulness always engenders loyalty. Betrayal or backstabbing is never an option for the one who is truly thankful and grateful.

Loyal for a Reason

Think deeply for a moment. At one time, Mary Magdalene was demonically possessed, which means she had neither the power nor the permission to do what she wanted to do. She was daily under the control of seven demons, and she marched to their beat and orders—not her own.

In my in-depth study of demonic possession, I discovered that Jesus delivered many demon-possessed people; however, none of those people came to Him on their own for deliverance. They were brought to Him, He went to them, or He called them to Himself (Matthew 8:16, 28, 29; 9:32; 12:22; Mark 9:20;

A Faithful Follower

Luke 13:12). Demons mentioned in Scripture always stayed as far away from Christ as possible. Moreover, they also kept the person whom they had possessed as far away from Christ as possible (Mark 1:23, 24; Luke 4:34; 8:26; Mark 9:20). These Scripture references reveal that Mary Magdalene did not search for Jesus to exorcise her demons because no demon (or demons) would ever allow a vessel they possessed to commit such treason. Therefore, either someone brought Mary Magdalene to Jesus or Jesus sought Mary Magdalene because she possessed neither the power nor the permission to seek Him. More than likely, Jesus pursued her.

He went to where she was at and where she was at certainly wasn't a church setting. I imagine it was more like a dark, deep pit that contained everything from A to Z. Her past was there. All her hurt and pain was there. Her demonic possession and every issue that came along with it were there. Believe me, nothing pretty was in that pit. Yet Jesus showed up there, and He pulled her up and out of that pit with a power much greater than any number of demons! Jesus met Mary Magdalene where she was at—amid the mess and misery, and He gave her a ministry. He gave her a mission and meaning! He gave her a reason to live and go on! How could she not be loyal to Him? How could she not be a faithful follower of His?

Much Forgiveness Equals Much Love

Those who have been forgiven much love much. Those who have been forgiven little love little. That's what Jesus said to Simon the Pharisee in reference to the mystery woman with the alabaster box of ointment who washed Jesus' feet with her tears, wiped them with her hair, kissed them, and anointed them with the ointment (Luke 7:36-47). Though there's no reason or Biblical support for believing that Mary Magdalene and the woman with the alabaster box are one and the same person as some erroneously teach, both women do have something in common. Like the woman with the alabaster box had been forgiven much and loved much, so had Mary Magdalene. And her love for Christ was communicated in several ways, one of them being loyalty.

All the Way and Beyond

Mary Magdalene's love and loyalty toward Christ was so great that she followed Him faithfully from the time of her conversion until the time of His crucifixion and beyond. Mary Magdalene loved Jesus so much that she remained loyal to Him when others began to display hatred and hostility toward Him. The thought of reneging on Him never crossed her committed mind. Mary Magdalene was devoted and determined to be there for Jesus like He had been there for her.

Visible Proof of Her Loyalty and Love

Luke writes in his gospel that Mary Magdalene along with Joanna, Susanna, and many others *"ministered unto him* [Jesus] *of their substance"* (Luke 8:2, 3, KJV). The fact that Mary Magdalene's name appears first in the list of women disciples more than likely means she was the leader of the group and held a significant and special role of respect and honor among them.

A Faithful Follower

The word for *ministered* in the Greek language is *diakoneo*, which means "to contribute, serve, wait upon, or take care of." The word *substance*, which is translated *huparcho* in the Greek, refers to "property, possession, belongings, and all that a person owns; also to one's life, one's being, and how one lives or behaves."

By connecting the definitions of the two words in their original language, a picture of devoted discipleship can be seen unfolding. Mary Magdalene, along with the other women, served and took care of Jesus, not by simply giving Him their property, possessions, or finances, but most importantly, by giving Him their lives and by living for Him. You cannot get more loyal than that! To submit and surrender your entire being and every behavior to someone is ultimate loyalty at its best.

As I stated at the beginning of this chapter, Mary Magdalene was loyal to the core. That loyalty led her to surrender her life and livelihood to Jesus. I would like to suggest that Mary Magdalene's loyalty to Jesus was manifested in at least three ways: through her time, her talents, and her treasures. Mary Magdalene proved her loyalty to the One who had liberated her by love. I want to concentrate on each of these loyalty traits individually.

Her Time

As Mary Magdalene ministered to Jesus with her time, she spent both quality and quantity time with Jesus. She spent a tremendous amount of meaningful time with Jesus. According to the passage found in Luke chapter eight, Mary Magdalene was alongside of the twelve disciples following Jesus as He went through every city and village in Galilee, preaching and showing good tidings of the kingdom of God. To follow Jesus means that where He went, she went and what He did, she did. Following Him is only possible by spending an abundance of time with Him.

Interestingly, every time Mary Magdalene's name is mentioned in Scripture, somehow the mention is always in relation to Jesus. This relationship only confirms that her time was no longer *her* time; it was *His* time. And Mary was willing to do with His time whatever Jesus needed or wanted her to do. She simply wanted to be in His presence.

She simply wanted to spend time with Him, doing those things that pleased Him—not herself. Someone once said, "Another spelling of love is T-I-M-E." That quote aptly explains that Mary Magdalene loved Jesus; therefore, she wanted to spend as much time with Him as possible. I personally find her willingness to give her time so freely very convicting.

Her Talents

Another way Mary Magdalene ministered to Jesus was with her talents. This statement is accurate because one of the definitions for *substance* in the Greek language is "being," and talents are a part of our being. We are born with them. As a result, we can be sure that whatever talent or talents Mary Magdalene had, she used them to minister to Jesus. Rather than sit on them, she surrendered them to His use. If her talent was singing, she sang; if it was organizing, she organized; if it was helping, she helped; if it was speaking, she spoke; if it was writing, she wrote. Mary Magdalene used what she had within her being to minister unto the Lord and magnify His name. Mary was a faithful steward over the gifts God had given her by His grace.

Her Treasures

The other way Mary Magdalene ministered to Jesus was through her treasures. Again, bear in mind, the definition of *substance* in the Scripture's original language also meant "possessions, property, and belongings." Treasures or finances obviously would fall under the category of substance, which means exactly what you think it means. Mary Magdalene supported Jesus financially by using her money and materials to support His ministry.

I believe financial support is the biggest test of loyalty. What you do or don't do with your money shows to whom or what you are loyal. Jesus said, *"For where your treasure is, there will your heart be also"* (Matthew 6:21, KJV). We know where Mary Magdalene's treasure was; consequently, we also know where her heart was. Both were safe and secure in the hands of Him who delivered her out of her dungeon of darkness and despair through His divine grace and goodness. YOU GO, MARY!

A Slight Switch of Focus

Mary Magdalene was a devoted disciple who faithfully followed her Lord and Savior Jesus Christ and ministered to Him from her time, talents, and treasures. That statement is not even up for debate. So allow me to switch the focus for a minute from her to you. How are *you* using your time, talents, and treasures? Are you using them to minister to the Lord and serve Him faithfully? If not, then why not? You may not be aware of this, but how you use your time, talents, and treasures proves or disproves your loyalty to Jesus. What you say with your lips doesn't prove your loyalty; what you say with your life does.

In April 1521, Martin Luther appeared before his ecclesiastical accusers at the Diet of the Worms. His indicters had issued him a final ultimatum to repudiate his unwavering faith in the supremacy and sufficiency of Scripture. Luther responded:

> *Unless I am* convicted by scripture and plain reason— I do not accept the authority of popes and councils, for they have contradicted each other—my conscience is captive to the Word of God. I cannot and I will not recant anything, for to go against conscience is neither right nor safe. God help me!...Here I stand.[2]

When all odds were against him, Martin Luther displayed loyalty to the Scriptures and to his Savior. May the same be said of us. May we leave behind us a legacy that is loaded with loyalty to the Scriptures and to the Savior.

I want to conclude this chapter up by sharing a stanza from the hymn, "From Pray'r that Asks that I May Be" written by Amy Carmichael:

Give me the love that leads the way,
The faith that nothing can dismay,

A Faithful Follower

The hope no disappointment tire,
The passion that will burn like fire,
Let me not sink to be a clod:
Make me Thy fuel, O flame of God.

May Amy's words become our words in a sincere prayer uttered to our God. My heart's desire is to fall among the ranks of Mary Magdalene, Martin Luther, and many others, and be noted as a loyal and faithful follower of the Lord Jesus Christ. Is it yours?

---

[2]Roland Herbert Banton, *Here I Stand: A Life of Martin Luther* (Peabody, Mass.: Hendrickson Publishers, 2009), 180.

CHAPTER FOUR

SOLD-OUT OR SELLOUT

"Then He said to them, "Follow Me, and I will make you fishers of men" (Matthew 4:19).

I WAS SITTING IN Saturday afternoon Bible class when the question was first presented to me. The minister of the hour was an elderly Caucasian man named Bill Robinson. The question he presented from behind the pulpit was, "If you were accused for the crime of being a disciple of Jesus, would the court find enough evidence to convict you and find you guilty?"

That question started the wheels in my mind to turning. Eventually, Bill's question gave birth to this question: What type of evidence is solid enough to prove beyond a reasonable doubt that a person is a disciple of Jesus? As I thought about how Scripture addresses the subject of discipleship and what Mary Magdalene's life teaches about discipleship, I see at least three pieces of evidence that constitute discipleship that I want to share in this chapter. However, before looking at the evidence, it would seem wise to obtain a Biblical definition of *disciple*. What exactly is a disciple?

Discipleship on Display

Much like Mary Magdalene, a *disciple* is "a faithful follower of a rabbi, teacher, or scholar. A *disciple* is basically "a pupil or learner." According to the *Holman Illustrated Bible Dictionary*,

> In the Greek World, the word *disciple* normally referred to an adherent of a particular teacher or religious philosophical school. It was the task of the disciple to learn, study, and pass along the sayings and teachings of the master. Through a process of learning which would include a set meeting time and such pedagogical methods as question and answer, instruction, repetition, and memorization, the disciple would become increasingly devoted to the master and the master's teaching.[3]

But that Bible dictionary definition is not all inclusive. The goal of a disciple was not only to learn what the teacher knew and teach it, the goal of the disciple was to become like the teacher (Luke 6:40). This was certainly the case when it came to Mary Magdalene and the other disciples of Jesus. The Savior's goal was to teach them; their goal was to learn from Him and become like Him in every sense of the word.

The same is true for disciples of Jesus today. His goal is to teach us, and our goal should be to learn from Him and become like Him in every sense of the word. This means that we, along with every other disciple of Jesus, must possess certain traits. At the beginning of the chapter, I called these traits *evidence*. I now want to look at the evidence that constitutes discipleship to discover what being a disciple of Jesus truly means.

At the same time, we will see that Mary Magdalene possessed these pieces of evidence, proving that she was a disciple of Jesus beyond a reasonable doubt.

The Evidence of Cross Bearing

The first piece of evidence that proves discipleship has to do with carrying a cross. Luke writes:

> *"Now great multitudes went with Him. And He turned and said to them, "If anyone comes to Me and does not hate his father and mother, wife and children, brothers and sisters, yes, and his own life also, he cannot be My disciple, And whoever does not bear his cross and come after Me cannot be My disciple"* (Luke 14:25-27).

Jesus' goal was to produce genuine disciples. With the great multitudes following Him, Jesus had to set the bar high in order to separate the committed followers from those who were not committed. Jesus wasn't the least bit interested in having a big group of half-hearted, fair-weather followers. In order to separate them, He made bold demands that were hard for the grouping to digest.

Jesus always declared the high cost of discipleship to discourage the wishy-washy followers. No doubt that's the reason for His bold demands found in Luke 14. In this passage, Jesus called for those who desired to be genuine disciples to take up their cross and follow Him. This call to life-or-death commitment to Christ is repeated over and over in the Gospels (Matthew 10:38; 16:24; Mark 8:34; Luke 9:23).

At the time, those who heard Jesus mention "carrying a cross" or "bearing a cross," it would have automatically painted a picture in their minds of a violent, heinous, debasing, merciless death. By making such a statement, Jesus was demanding from the hearers of His words a total commitment—even one to death! Cross bearing, therefore, was and is a call to suffer, sacrifice, and surrender all. It's a call to deny self for the sake of Christ and the furtherance of His kingdom. Following this call means every personal relationship (Luke 14:26), personal goal and plan (Luke 14:27), and personal possession (Luke 14:33) must be surrendered under the Lordship of Jesus Christ. A refusal to do so means a person cannot be a disciple of Jesus. Either He's Lord of all or He isn't Lord at all!

A Demand to Hate

When it comes to cross bearing, Jesus unilaterally uses the term *hate* (Luke 14:26), indicating that part of cross bearing is that a disciple hates his closest family members and his own life as well.

On the surface, this requisite seems like a contradiction to the very values and principles of Christianity; that is, until we understand that the term for *hate* used by Jesus means to "love less." Jesus calls for His disciples to love everyone and everything else less fervently in comparison to their love for Him. This requirement is seen more clearly in Matthew 10:37 when Jesus said: *"He who loves father or mother more than Me is not worthy of Me. And he who loves son or daughter more than Me is not worthy of Me."* Jesus expects every disciple to invest all in Him and forsake all for Him. He expects a total surrender and a renunciation of every person, privilege, and possession that competes against the making of such commitment.

Moreover, the renunciation that Jesus calls for must be without reservation. For that reason, Jesus said several times in the Gospels (Matthew 10:39, Mark 8:35, Luke 9:24, Luke 17:33, John 12:25) that *"...whoever desires to save his life will lose it, but whoever loses his life for My sake will find it"* (Matthew 16:25). Indeed, this principle is paradoxical; nevertheless, the fact that it is a principle still holds true! Those who refuse to renounce and let go, lose out in the end. They cling and cling until they lose everything. Whereas, those who let go and surrender all gain more than they ever had before, with eternal life being number one on the list!

Corrie Ten Boom said, "Hold everything in your hands lightly, otherwise it hurts when God pries your fingers open."[4] Such wise words—especially for a disciple. Hold things loosely! Totally surrender all to Jesus! Don't hold out one single thing! Don't hold on to any of it! Let it all go! Relinquishing everything is what Jesus desires and demands of His disciple. And unless a person is ready to go to that extreme, he cannot be a disciple of Jesus. To make it more personal, unless you and I are ready and willing to go to that extreme and lose our lives like Mary Magdalene and a few faithful others did, then neither can we be a disciple of Jesus.

J-O-Y

From time to time, this simple acronym of the word "joy" has helped me to keep my priorities straight, which in turn, helps me to bear my cross daily. J-O-Y is an acrostic for **Jesus**, **Others**, and **Yourself**—in that order When Jesus speaks of bearing a cross, all that He is really saying is "Put Me first, put others second and yourself last." When we choose to follow that order, then and only then are we displaying evidence of being a disciple of Jesus.

Counting the Cost

After Jesus talked to the great multitude about cross bearing, He went right to the heart of the matter—the subject of counting the cost.

> *"For which of you, intending to build a tower, does not sit down first and count the cost, whether he has enough to finish it—lest, after he has laid the foundation, and is not able to finish, all who see it begin to mock him, saying, 'This man began to build and was not able to finish'. Or what king, going to make war against another king, does not sit down first and consider whether he is able with ten thousand to meet him who comes against him with twenty thousand? Or else, while the other is still a great way off, he sends a delegation and asks conditions of peace. So likewise, whoever of you does not forsake all that he has cannot be My disciple"* (Luke 14:28-33).

Jesus has given His audience two scenarios. One has to do with a man who intends to build a tower; the other has to do with a king's going to war against another king. The point that Jesus was making by explaining the two scenarios has to do with the need for counting the cost before committing to a cause. Jesus was saying like the man needed to count the cost before building a tower and the king needed to count the cost before going to war, every potential disciple needs to count the cost before simply jumping up and attempting to halfheartedly follow Him. Jesus, through the proclamation of the two scenarios, was encouraging the multitudes to do an inventory or a careful consideration before making their willingness to follow Him publicly known.

Jesus wanted them to really think about the commitment. He wanted them to weigh their options, to look at the pros and cons, and to consider whether the sacrifice was worth it before they made a decision that would forever change their lives. Unfortunately, some thought about it and didn't think the sacrifice was worth it (Matthew 8:18-22; Matthew 19:16-22; Luke 9:57-62). Sadly, even today, there are those who do not think cross bearing is worth the sacrifice.

As Pastor Paul Shepherd once explained in his creative, unique style of preaching, "Satan reminds us of what it cost to follow Jesus, but he never reminds us of how much it pays." May I remind you of how much it pays? The pay is much greater than the cost. The gain is much greater than the loss. In other words, it's worth it! When it comes to what we get versus what we give up, there's no comparison! *"For I consider that the sufferings of this present time are not worthy to be compared with the glory which shall be revealed in us"* (Romans 8:18). That's how the apostle Paul put it.

The Evidence of Bearing Fruit

A second piece of evidence that proves discipleship has to do with bearing fruit. In fact, a disciple of Jesus is expected to bear fruit. In John 15:8, Jesus said, *"By this My Father is glorified, that you bear much fruit; so you will be My disciples."*

The Scripture identifies three kinds of spiritual fruit:

1) Spiritual attitudes of a Spirit-filled believer (Galatians 5:22, 23)

2) Actions or works (Matthew 7:16-20; Romans 6:22; Philippians 4:16, 17; Hebrews 13:15)

3) Fruit of labor or new converts (Romans 1:13; 16:5; Philippians 1:22).

A disciple of Jesus is expected to bear all three kinds of fruit. He is expected to bear the fruit of the Spirit (love, joy, peace, longsuffering, kindness, goodness, faithfulness, gentleness, and self-control) in his attitude. He is expected to bear the fruit of good works and actions in his day-to-day living and activities. A disciple is also expected to bear the fruit of new converts through evangelizing and witnessing.

When a disciple of Jesus brings forth all three kinds of fruit, according to Jesus, two results occur. One, the Father is glorified. Two, the disciple who bears such fruit proves beyond a shadow of doubt that he is a disciple of Jesus.

At this point, consider again Mary Magdalene. Think about her level of character in the previous chapters. Did Mary bear any fruit? Let me answer that question for you. Yes, she certainly did!

The Evidence of Abiding

The third piece of evidence that proves discipleship has to do with abiding. A disciple of Jesus is expected to abide in Him. In fact, abiding in Christ is essential when it comes to bearing fruit. In an agricultural metaphor found in John 15 about vines, branches, and fruit, Jesus makes the point clear:

> *Abide in Me, and I in you. As the branch cannot bear fruit of itself, unless it abides in the vine, neither can you, unless you abide in Me. "I am the vine, you are the branches. He who abides in Me, and I in him, bears much fruit; for without Me you can do nothing"* (John 15:4, 5).

In short, Jesus was saying to His disciples as well as to us that unless we abide in Him, we cannot bear any fruit. Therefore, abiding in Jesus is not only expected, it's essential. A disciple cannot bear fruit apart from abiding in Jesus. The goal, according to Jesus' agricultural metaphor, is a progressive one—going from no fruit to fruit, from fruit to more fruit, and from more fruit to much fruit (John 15:2, 5). Again, such a goal is accomplished through abiding in Jesus.

The word *abides* means "to habitually remain or stay around; to continue." The word describes a person who has no thoughts or intentions of leaving Christ. He is sold out to his Savior, and the thought of selling out for the pleasure of the flesh or the ways of the world isn't even an option. Unless a disciple of Jesus continues with Jesus, he isn't a true disciple of Jesus.

The evidence of a disciple's being who he claims to be is whether he continues. If he doesn't continue, persevere or endure and if he doesn't finish the race that has been set before him, then he isn't who he claims to be. Those aren't my words; those are the words of Jesus Christ. He said cut and dried: *"...If you abide in My word, you are My disciples indeed"* (John 8:31).

The implication of this verse is if you don't abide, then you aren't His disciple. The apostle John expounded on this very truth in his letter to the churches in Asia Minor. John exercised apostolic leadership over these churches, and he wrote to them in such a fashion. Read thoughtfully what he wrote about those disciples who depart from the faith and fellowship and refuse to run on.

> *"They went out from us, but they were not of us; for if they had been of us, they would have continued with us; but they went out that they might be made manifest, that none of them were of us"* (1 John 2:19).

The truth of this verse is undeniable; a disciple who abandons the faith and the fellowship and doesn't continue isn't truly a disciple at all. According to John, they never were disciples, regardless of what they professed or proclaimed. Their actions manifested the truth, and the truth was they weren't of the fold. They were fake! They were phonies! They may have carried the name and spoke the language of a disciple, but if they had been genuine disciples, they would have faithfully and habitually remained with Jesus. Like Mary, they would have continued.

I often say, "Listen to a man, and he'll tell you anything. Watch him, and he'll show you everything." Those who say they are disciples will eventually show you whether or not they really are. A passage of Scripture found in John's gospel perfectly conveys the point I'm trying to relay:

> *Therefore many of His disciples, when they heard this, said, "This is a hard saying; who can understand it? When Jesus knew in Himself that His disciples complained about this, He said to them, "Does this offend you? "What then if you should see the Son of Man ascend where He was before? "It is the Spirit who gives life; the flesh profits nothing. The words that I speak to you are spirit, and they are life. But there are some of you who do not believe." For Jesus knew from the beginning who they were who did not believe, and who would betray Him. And He said, "Therefore I have said to you that no one can come to Me unless it has been granted to him by My Father." From that time many of His disciples went back and walked with Him no more. Then Jesus said unto the twelve, "Do you also want to go away?" But Simon Peter answered Him, "Lord, to whom shall we go? You have the words of eternal life. Also we have come to believe and know that You are the Christ, the Son of the Living God."*
> (John 6:60-69)

Phony Followers

In the previous passage, John lists two groups of disciples and their reaction to Jesus' sermon on the "The Bread of Life." Their reaction to His sermon proves their identity. After hearing the sermon, one group acknowledged that what Jesus had shared was too hard to handle (v. 60) and from that time, many of them went back and walked with Jesus no longer (v. 66). To begin with, these disciples were probably only following Jesus for all the wrong reasons. Quite possibly, they were attracted to the miracles, food, and the tangible goods. When those things sort of played out and the sayings got hard, their true colors came shining through. They made a conscious and final decision to desert Jesus, proving they were imitation disciples—fake from the beginning. These disciples showed Jesus who they were, or should I say, who they weren't. Remember that those who fade away in the finish were fake from the first.

The Real Deal

On the other hand, the second group of disciples showed who they were as well. After the abandonment by the other group, Jesus asked the twelve, "Do you also want to go away?" (v. 67).

Peter, answering for the twelve, replied with an answer that should represent the one that comes from the lips of every genuine disciple. Peter said, *"Lord, to whom shall we go? You have the words of eternal life. Also we have come to believe and know that You are the Christ, the Son of the Living God"* (vv. 68, 69). In total contrast with the first group of disciples' reactions, Peter's answer to Jesus' question proved that he, along with the others (except for Judas), were genuine disciples.

They had put their hand to the plow, and unlike the other group of disciples, they didn't have an inkling of a desire to look back or go back. Jesus said on one occasion, *"...No one, having put his hand to the plow, and looking back, is fit for the kingdom of God"* (Luke 9:62).

Staying Fit

Do you want to be considered fit for the kingdom of God? Then don't look back! Abide in Jesus! Habitually remain in Him! Stay around! Stick around! Starting is not enough; after all, many people start. But you, as well as I, must finish. We must continue to bear our cross, count the cost, and bring forth fruit. These traits are the evidence that constitutes discipleship, and such evidence must be displayed continually. In short, you cannot display the evidence for a while and then stop. The evidence that constitutes discipleship must continually come forth. There's no way around it. You and I must continue. We must abide!

The Evidence of Discipleship in Mary's Life

Did Mary Magdalene abide in Christ? Did she continue? Yes, she did! She did continue to carry her cross and count the cost. She did continue to bear fruit. She did continue to follow Jesus—all the way to the cross and beyond. Mary Magdalene wasn't a sellout; she was sold out, totally surrendered and completely committed to Jesus.

In closing this chapter, may I share a word of encouragement with you? If Mary Magdalene can be a diligent disciple, so can you! So can you!

A Prayer to Pray

Father in Heaven, we come humbly and boldly to Your throne of grace and mercy, expecting to find help in this time of need. We acknowledge that, apart from You, we are helpless, and life is hopeless. Apart from You, dear God, we can do nothing! This means that for us to be true, genuine disciples, we need Your help; we need Your power. The deep desire of our hearts is not only to learn from Jesus and teach Jesus but also to become like Jesus. We desire to become like Him in words, motives, thoughts, and deeds. Help us! Empower us!

As You know, Father, the spirit is willing, but the flesh is weak. The flesh wars against the spirit and always wants to have its way. But as You have instructed in Your Word, we crucify the flesh and make a conscious decision to surrender all to You today. We trust You to daily keep us in this place of surrender and to strip us of everything and everyone who would sway or lure us away from this place.

My prayer is that I, along with my other brothers and sisters in the faith, would be found guilty of being a true disciple of Jesus. And may the evidence of bearing our cross—bringing forth fruit, walking in love, and abiding in Jesus—be clearly and visibly seen in our lives today and every day. In the name of Jesus, I pray. Amen!

CHAPTER FIVE

WHAT'S LOVE GOT TO DO WITH IT?

"By this all will know that you are My disciples, if you have love for one another" (John 13:35).

Love. I'm convinced that this word has suffered more misuse and abuse than any other word within our English vocabulary. The word *love* in the last two centuries has been stripped and robbed of its true meaning and left powerless. The word has become so weakened and devalued throughout the years that people, both young and old, use it in reference to just about anything and everything. It's not uncommon in the least bit to hear statements such as, "I *love* my car," I *love* my house," "I *love* my job," "I *love* the Dallas Cowboys," and on and on it goes. Basically, these people are saying "I like the way this thing or these things make me feel," or "These things make me feel good, so I love them." But that's not love!

Love, in its fullest revelation, was never meant to be

based on superficial emotions or feelings that fluctuate like the wind—at least not according to Jesus or the Word of God. Neither has love ever been able to truly and fully express itself in words alone and apart from deeds (I John 3:18). According to Jesus and the Word of God, at the heart of this word *love* has always been a selfless act or acts that displays to its recipient that the giver has his best interest at heart.

A Love Without Limits

During the times and days of Jesus, the Greeks used four different words for that one word *love*: *eros* ("sexual love"), *phileo* ("friendship" or "brotherly love"), *storgē* ("family love"), and *agapé* ("unconditional love"). What I find interesting is that when Jesus dealt with His disciples about loving Him, others, and one another, He always used the same Greek word for love. He always used *agapé*, which says, "I haven't placed any conditions, limits, or stipulations on My love toward you, and I don't want those who are followers of Me to place any conditions, limits, or stipulations on their love toward Me, others, or one another."

Biblical love from the viewpoint of Jesus is a love without limits that goes above and beyond the call of duty. The bottom line motivator is that disciples of Jesus aren't simply called to *live* differently; they are called to *love* differently. Anyone can love until the one he love rubs him wrong or does something he doesn't approve of. The test of genuine love is its ability to love in spite of. To grant a love that is unmerited, undeserved, and unconditional is what Jesus has in mind for all His disciples. That viewpoint brings up a question that every disciple of Christ needs to specifically address: exactly who are to be the recipients of such a love as I've described? I find no less than three answers in Scripture to that question.

A Call to Love Our God

First, a disciple of Jesus is commanded to love God. In Matthew's gospel, a scribe from the sect of the Pharisees asked Jesus a question in order to test Him: *"Teacher, which is the great commandment in the law?"* (Matthew 22:36).

Jesus replied to His question by saying, *"You shall love the LORD your God with all your heart, with all your soul, and with all your mind. This is the first and great commandment"* (Matthew 22:37, 38). The command that Jesus issued that day goes all the way back to Deuteronomy 6:5. To love the Lord with all your heart, soul, and mind is to love Him completely and with one's entire being. A disciple of Jesus is commanded to love God in this way. God is first and foremost on the disciple's love list.

A Call to Love Our Neighbors

Second, a disciple of Jesus is commanded to love his neighbors. In the same account of Matthew's gospel, Jesus continued to address the scribe's trick question by adding, *"And the second is like it: 'You shall love your neighbor as yourself.' On these two commandments hang all the law and the prophets"* (Matthew 22:39, 40). This commandment was also an Old Testament quotation found in Leviticus 19:18.

Woman, Why Weepest Thou?

In no uncertain terms, Jesus made known to all who were listening at the time the importance of loving their neighbor. He ranked it right up there with loving God, and then He adds on these two commands (loving God and loving neighbors) hang all the law and the prophets. What exactly was Jesus saying? He was saying that when a man properly loves God and his neighbor, he fulfills the Law, more specifically, the Ten Commandments.

If a man loves God with all his heart, soul, and mind, he will not violate the first four of the Ten Commandments, which address an individual's personal relationship with God. Likewise, if a man loves his neighbor as he loves himself, he will not violate the last six of the Ten Commandments, which deal with an individual's personal relationship and interaction with others. Apparently, the apostle Paul had this relationship in mind when he wrote the following to the church in Rome:

> *Owe no one anything except love one another, for he who loves another fulfilled the law. For the commandments, "You shall not commit adultery," "You shall not murder," "You shall not steal," "You shall not bear false witness," "You shall not covet," and if there is any other commandment, are summed up in this saying, namely, "You shall love your neighbor as yourself." Love does no harm to a neighbor; therefore love is the fulfillment of the law* (Romans 13:8-10).

No wonder Jesus commanded those who were His faithful followers to love, which fulfills the law and is the foundation and framework of every command and every Scripture. And when we get love right, we get the rest right—but not until!

A Call to Love Our Enemies

Disciples of Jesus are called to love God and their neighbors. But another group of people also fall under the heading of *neighbors* that I must mention. Of course, I am referring to enemies. Unfortunately, all neighbors aren't lovable and likeable. Some will be enemies who hate and despise us with a passion. These people are the most difficult to love, yet a disciple of Jesus is called to love them the same. What did Jesus say concerning this touchy subject?

> *"You have heard it was said, 'You shall love your neighbor and hate your enemy.' But I say to you, love your enemies, bless those who curse you, do good to those who hate you, and pray for those who spitefully use you and persecute you, that you may be sons of your Father in Heaven; for He makes the sun shine on the evil and on the good, and sends rain on the just and on the unjust. For if you love those who love you, what reward have you? Do not even the tax collectors do the same?"*
> (Matthew 5:43-46)

Jesus makes it quite clear that His followers must operate in a love so divine that it extends to the very ones who hate and misuse us. To do otherwise puts us in the category of the tax collectors of Jesus' day and robs us of our rewards. Though I cannot think of anyone who deserves to be less loved than a person's enemies, I believe the whole point is to pour out love on the people who deserve it the least. After all, isn't that what God did for us? In his letter to the believers in Corinth, the apostle Paul was inspired by the Holy Spirit to record verses that are worthy of memorization:

> *"For the love of Christ compels us, because we judge thus: that if One died for all, then all died; and He died for all, that those who live should live no longer for themselves, but for Him who died for them and rose again."*
> (2 Corinthians 5:14, 15)

When we live no longer for ourselves, but for Him who died for us and rose again, we are compelled by His love to reach out to others in love, including our enemies.

A Call to Love One Another

Third, a disciple of Jesus is commanded to love other believers. In John's gospel, Jesus cuts no corners concerning this issue. In a conversation about His upcoming departure, Jesus began explaining to His disciples what He expected of them after He left. What was His subject of choice? Love.

> *"A new commandment I give to you, that you love one another; as I have loved you, that you also love one another. By this all will know that you are My disciples, if you have love for one another"* (John 13:34, 35).

This commandment to love was not new in the sense of never existing. We established earlier that the commandment to love can be traced all the way back to the Old Testament. So, what exactly did Jesus mean when He used the words, *"new commandment"*?

When Jesus used the phrase, *"new commandment,"* He was referring to *new* in the sense of "a new kind." Jesus' disciples were to love one another in a new kind of way. A distinct and new standard was about to be established. They were to love one another exactly like Jesus had loved them. In other words, they were to follow His example of sacrificial love. According to 1 John 3:16, they were to lay down their lives for one another.

"By this we know love, because He laid down His life for us. And we also ought to lay down our lives for the brethren" (1 John 3:16).

The Power to Pull It Off

The commandment was new also in the sense that Jesus' disciples would be expressing such a love for one another through a new covenant by the power of the Holy Spirit as He poured out the love of God in their hearts (Jeremiah 31:31-34; Ezekiel 36:24-27; Romans 5:5; Galatians 5:22). A very important point needs to be established as it relates to the love being addressed in this chapter. The point is that loving someone with the love of God apart from the Spirit of God is impossible.

The type of love with which we are called to love our God, our neighbors, our enemies, and our brothers and sisters cannot be mustered up in our own strength. That kind of love must be perfected through the power of the Holy Spirit. No wonder that after Jesus' resurrection He told these same disciples and others that He was going to send the promise of His Father upon them, and they were to tarry in Jerusalem until they were imbued with power from on high (Luke 24:49; Acts 1:4-8). Jesus knew that they, as well as every other disciple, would need that power of the Holy Spirit to love and witness effectively!

The Proof Is in the Pudding

Here, then, is the complete truth concerning the whole matter: the love that Jesus expected His disciples to love one another with was to be both sacrificial and supernatural. According to Jesus, the expression of that love on other believers is the distinguishing evidence of discipleship. Loving one another is the primary proof to the world around us that we are indeed disciples of Jesus. On the contrary, if we do not love one another, if we do not love our neighbors and enemies, and if we do not love our God, then what does that prove?

What Love Does

At the beginning of the chapter, I briefly touched on this topic, but the subject needs to be addressed in detail before concluding this chapter. If love proves discipleship, then it's imperative to understand what love does. The word *does* is the key word. Love does something and is always doing something. Love doesn't simply sit back and twiddle its thumbs, making mere proclamations. Love in its truest, purest form is an action—not an abstraction. It isn't enough for me to say, "I love you." On the contrary, I must show that person that I love him or her.

And showing that love can only be done through one's actions. The scripture repeatedly reminds us that love does something; it doesn't sit idly by and make announcements of love apart from deeds of love. The apostle John, also known as "the disciple of love" admonished the recipients of his letter concerning this exact same subject as well:

> *"My little children, let us not love in word or in tongue, but in deed and in truth"* (1 John 3:18).

Claiming to love is not enough! A person's actions must support his claim or his claim is in vain. In fact, Paul, the legendary apostle, wrote an entire chapter about love in his letter to the Corinthian church. In this chapter on love, Paul does an excellent job of conveying the message of love as being an action word:

> *"Love never gives up. Love cares more for others than for self. Love doesn't want what it doesn't have. Love doesn't strut. Doesn't have a swelled head, doesn't force itself on others, isn't always "me first," doesn't fly off the handle, doesn't keep score of the sins of others, doesn't revel when others grovel, takes pleasure in the flowering of truth, puts up with anything, trusts God always, always looks for the best, never looks back, but keeps going to the end. Love never dies..."* (1 Corinthians 13:4-8, MSG).

Get the message? Love is fluid—always doing, always moving, and always giving. Love is an action word. In order to summarize and simplify, allow me to offer to share three ways love displays itself: love reaches up, over, and out.

Love reaches *up* to God in adoration, in praise, in worship, in reverence, in prayer, in submission, and in obedience. Love reaches up to God.

Love reaches *over* racial barriers, gender barriers, religious barriers, political barriers, social barriers, and cultural barriers. Love reaches over all types of barriers.

Love reaches *out* to those who are left out—the outcasts and the cast out, friends and foes, brothers and sisters. Love never looks down on or turns up its nose at the individuals whom society has ridiculed, spurned and rejected. Love reaches out—far out! To connect the dots, love reaches up to God in order to reach over barriers so that it can reach out to our neighbors, enemies, and fellow believers. Understand? Great!

Follow the Leader

As always, Jesus, who was love personified, is our example and pattern to follow. During His entire earthly ministry, He demonstrated His love for the Father and others by reaching up, reaching over, and reaching out. Jesus always reached up to His Heavenly Father in adoration, praise, prayer, submission, and obedience. He constantly made statements about not seeking His own will, but the will of the Father that had sent Him (John 5:30; 6:38). Throughout His entire earthly ministry, Jesus also always reached over all types of racial, social, religious, political, gender, and cultural barriers in order to influence fishermen, zealots, tax collectors, Samaritans, prostitutes, and demoniacs. When it comes to how love reaches up, over, and out, Jesus is our perfect example to follow. May we follow Him with a heart of passion and obedience!

What About Mary Magdalene?

If your mind works like mine, you have to be wondering, "What about Mary Magdalene? Where does she fit in?" Like a newly released color to be added to an assorted box of crayons, Mary Magdalene fits in perfectly!

Though the Bible does not plainly state that Mary Magdalene loved her neighbors, her enemies, and other believers, the word of God certainly tells us and shows us that she loved Jesus with all her heart, soul, and mind. She proved her love by how she devoted her time, talents, and treasures to Him. Based on her love for Him, I am more than convinced that she displayed love for her neighbors, her enemies, and other believers as well. Jesus said, *"If you love Me, keep My commandments"* (John 14:15).

Jesus also said, *"He who has My commandments and keeps them, it is he who loves Me...If anyone loves Me, he will keep My word..."* (John 14:21, 23). In these verses, Jesus is saying that the proof of a person's love for Him is whether that person obeys His commandments.

Some of Jesus' very commandments were to love our neighbors, enemies, and other believers. Therefore, since Mary Magdalene loved Jesus, I believe she would have happily kept and obeyed those commandments and displayed love for her neighbors, enemies, and fellow believers. When considering all the facts, a conclusion can be safely drawn that Mary Magdalene's love life was fully intact. She loved Jesus, and those who love Jesus obey Him. Those who obey Jesus love their neighbors, their enemies, and their brothers and sisters in the faith.

In fact, a Scripture found in the epistle of 1 John deals

precisely with the subject of love, especially as it relates to believers' loving other believers. I hope and trust that these verses will cause you to examine yourself and stimulate a greater desire within your heart to love the Creator and all His creation more fervently and passionately.

> *If someone says, "I love God" and hates his brother, he is a liar; for he who does not love his brother whom he has seen, how can he love God whom he hath not seen? And this commandment we have from Him; that he who loves God must love his brother also"* (1 John 4:20, 21).

The most appropriate question to ask now is "How's your love life?" Please don't respond too quickly. Let the question really register. Take the time to really look at your love life and see how it measures up to Jesus' commands. That, after all, is the whole reason for this chapter.

Points to Ponder

We could easily make the transition from chapter five to chapter six without pausing to ponder. We certainly don't need an intermission period…or do we? Enough has certainly been stated about love…or has it? The truth is we need this break in between chapters to be able to pause and ponder a point of great value.

By now, you have likely surmised that the point to ponder has to do with love. Let me state it so you can ponder its truth: Love covers over, but love doesn't cover up.

1 Peter 4:8 says, *And above all things have fervent love for*

What's Love Got to Do with It?

one another, for "love will cover a multitude of sins." The word *fervent* means "to be stretched" or "to be strained." The word paints a picture of a runner who is moving at maximum output with tight muscles being strained and stretched to the limit. This illustration pictures the kind of love that Christians are commanded to love one another with. However, that is not the point I want to focus on from the verse.

I am more interested in the latter half of the verse: *"...love will cover a multitude of sins."* This portion of Scripture interests me because we who are pouring out our love on others need to know the difference between "covering *up* sin" and "covering *over* sin." Real love *covers over* sin; real love *never covers up* sin! This means, in the area of personal offenses, the one who was offended should look over the offense if possible and be quick to show mercy and grant forgiveness. Love covers over sins with a blanket of grace, mercy, and forgiveness.

On the other hand, this verse does not mean personal or public offenses can be ignored, nor can a blind eye be turned, pretending nothing has happened. Love never covers up sin. In other words, love cares enough to confront and tell an individual the truth. Love apart from truth is questionable love. If you love someone, you love them enough to tell them the truth.

Paul the apostle exhorted the believers in Ephesus to "speak the truth in love" (Ephesians 4:15). He also exhorted them to "put away lying and speak truth with their neighbor" (Ephesians 4:25). Pastor Paul Shepherd wisely addressed this matter with the following statement: "Love apart from truth isn't reality, and truth apart from love is brutality."

Truth and love work hand in hand together, compensating one another. So if you truly love that spouse, that child, that parent, that friend, that neighbor, that sibling…then love them enough to tell them the truth. Believe me, the chances are considerable that you will be thanked for it—either then or later.

Under the inspiration of the Holy Spirit, the wise preacher, Solomon, once wrote:

> *"Open rebuke is better than love carefully concealed. Faithful are the wounds of a friend, but the kisses of an enemy are deceitful"* (Proverbs 27:5, 6).

> *"He who rebukes a man will find more favor afterward than he who flatters with the tongue"* (Proverbs 28:23).

Once again, this is the point to ponder: love covers *over* sin, but love doesn't cover *up* sin. Don't merely ponder the point; apply the point. Start today because there is no time like the present.

---

[3] Chad Brand and Eric Mitchell, Editors, *Holman Illustrated Bible Dictionary* (Nashville: Holman Reference, 2015), 165.

[4] Debbie McDaniel, "40 Powerful Quotes from Corrie Ten Boom," *Crosswalk.com*, http://www.crosswalk.com/faith/spiritual-life/inspiring-quotes/40-powerful-quotes-from-corrie-ten-boom.html, accessed 26 May 2107.

Part Four
Disappointment

"Life's not fair!" You hear it everywhere—on the playground, the athletic field, in the office, in the entertainment world, in the medical arena, even in the Bible. As a pastor, I have heard these words more often than I care to think. Lawyers, spouses, children, students…you name it, no one has been immune from the feelings of injustice. Life's unfairness touches everyone at one time or another.

– ROBERT SCHULLER

CHAPTER SIX

THE WORST WEEKEND EVER

"Now there stood by the cross of Jesus His mother, and His mother's sister, Mary the wife of Clopas, and Mary Magdalene" (John 19:25).

A FAVORITE POEM of mine, which was penned by Robert Browning Hamilton, speaks of the lack of fulfillment and dissatisfaction that comes with pleasure as opposed to the knowledge, wisdom, and understanding gained from going through rough and rugged places.

> I walked a mile with Pleasure;
> She chatted all the way;
> But left me none the wiser
> For all she had to say.
>
> I walked a mile with Sorrow;
> And ne'er a word said she;
> But, oh! The things I learned from her
> When Sorrow walked with me.
> — ROBERT BROWNING HAMILTON

Woman, Why Weepest Thou?

Discipleship on Display

Mary Magdalene's life thus far can be separated into three stages: 1) Her demons, 2) Her deliverance, and 3) Her devotion. At this point in examining her life, Mary Magdalene is now an official, devoted disciple of Jesus Christ. She has been freed from her own private prison so that she can faithfully follow the One who liberated her by love. Mary Magdalene's plans and purpose in life are now bigger and brighter than ever before. There is, however, something about discipleship that Mary must learn firsthand through experience: discipleship comes with a certain amount of hardship.

I am quite sure that on several occasions Mary Magdalene heard Jesus talk about how disciples must count the cost and take up their cross and follow Him. I am more than certain that she heard Jesus talk multiple times about how a disciple is called to suffer. Still, to hear about suffering is one thing; to experience suffering is totally another matter.

An Unpopular Truth

The truth is that every disciple of Jesus Christ must listen to Him, be led by Him, and learn from Him. The unpopular and often unspoken part of that truth is that one of the main ways a disciple learns from Jesus is by going through sorrowful and difficult times. The sweet psalmist of Israel proudly proclaimed, *"It is good for me that I have been afflicted, that I may learn Your statues"* (Psalm 119:71). Remember the second stanza of the poem by Mr. Hamilton at the beginning of this chapter?

> I walked a mile with Sorrow;
> And ne'er a word said she;
> But, oh! The things I learned from her
> When Sorrow walked with me.

Jesus' disciples are taught by Him and learn from Him during sorrowful and sad times! In other words, every disciple must take a required course in disappointments, and that course is not an elective.

Experientially, Mary Magdalene did not know this truth, but she was about to learn it firsthand. Though she wasn't aware of it at the time, life was on the verge of throwing Mary Magdalene an unwelcomed and unexpected curve ball.

An Unexpected Twist

Mary Magdalene had faithfully followed Jesus everywhere—through cities, crowds, communities, and even controversy, but now her love and loyalty would compel her to follow Him somewhere she wasn't expecting to go—to Calvary and the Cross.

In his gospel, John writes that Mary Magdalene along with three other women *"...stood by the cross of Jesus"* (John 19:25). To stand by the cross indicates that Mary Magdalene was near the cross, which means she would have certainly heard and seen some of the most gross and gruesome details of Jesus' crucifixion.

I believe Mary Magdalene would have seen and smelled the blood of Jesus as it dripped and dropped from His limp and almost lifeless body. She would have seen the crowd strike Him and spit on Him. She would have heard the crowd mock Him and ridicule Him. She would have heard Him cry out, *"Eli, Eli, lama sabachthani?" that is My God, My God, why have You forsaken Me?"* (Matthew 27:46). Mary Magdalene would have heard Him say, *"I thirst"* (John 19:28), and *"It is finished!"* (John 19:30). She would have seen Him bow His head and give up the Ghost and even more.

Another fact worth mentioning is that John records Mary Magdalene as standing by the cross, but Matthew and Mark record Mary Magdalene as "looking on from afar" (Matthew 27:55; Mark 15:40). Apparently, these verses describe a progression that took place at the Cross.

What I believe transpired is that as the suffering of her Savior became more intense and inhumane and as the scene became uglier, nastier, and bloodier, Mary Magdalene, along with the other women, naturally began to pull back. The scene was too horrific for them to watch up close any longer. As one commentator perfectly stated, "She couldn't bear to watch, but she couldn't bear to leave."

A Hard Pill to Swallow

This weekend had to have been by far Mary Magdalene's worst ever! Can you even imagine what was going on in her head and heart? Can you imagine what Mary was experiencing? One word comes to my mind: *disappointment!* How she must have been disappointed with the religious leaders and the crowd for crucifying her Lord! How disappointed she must

Woman, Why Weepest Thou?

have been with God for seemingly sitting on His hands and letting the whole sequence of events happen! How disappointed she must have been with herself for being helpless when it came to helping the One who had helped her so much! After all Jesus had done for her, she couldn't do anything for Him. That powerlessness and inadequacy must have hurt more than everything else combined.

My goal is not to send you into an emotional frenzy; rather, my goal for you is to try putting yourself in Mary Magdalene's shoes. See life from her perspective. Mary Magdalene is watching as the King of kings is being killed. She is looking on as the Messiah is being murdered. But for Mary Magdalene, what she was watching was much more personal and deeper than that. She wasn't watching just any king or any Messiah; this was her King and her Messiah! Mary's Deliverer was dying, along with her dreams, and she could do absolutely nothing to prevent it from happening. As the age-old idiom states, *her hands were tied*. Standing by and having no way to intervene on the behalf of her Savior had to be a very hard pill for her to swallow.

Talk about a bad day or bad timing! When life had started looking up for Mary Magdalene and when she thought she had plenty time to grow her faith and get to know Jesus, the bottom fell out of her life. The blues fell in. When everything seemed to be coming together and beginning to look like as though all would work out fine, the rug was snatched from under her feet. No doubt, Mary Magdalene was left with a plethora of questions and not many answers. No wonder she was disappointed; I believe you would have been too.

Woman, Why Weepest Thou?

The truth is, we have all been where Mary was at the foot of the cross. Right when it looked like the marriage would survive or the business would thrive or the rebellious runaway was headed home or the cancer was in remission or the foreclosure on the home would be prevented or the friendship would be restored, an unexpected turn of events transpired, leaving us perplexed and perturbed. Like Mary, we were left disappointed with others and with God, but most of all, with ourselves for being so naive and foolish enough to believe and hope for something bigger and brighter.

As I work on this manuscript, I find myself in a place like Mary's. Without going into all of the details, I will simply say that I had prayed and fasted earnestly about a situation, and I had expected a specific answer. But when the answer came, the solution did not come exactly as I had expected it to come. The answer didn't unfold and unravel in the way I was hoping. The result was disappointment—disappointment with God, others, and me.

This resulting disappointment led me to look through my collection of poems. I found one whose author is unknown that is distributed by Joni and friends that vividly and accurately describes how God takes disappointments and uses them to mold and make a man or a woman.

> *When God wants* to drill a man, and thrill a man and skill a man,
> When God wants to mold a man to play the noblest part,

The Worst Weekend Ever

> When He yearns with all His heart to create so great
>   and bold a man
> That all the world shall be amazed,
> Watch His methods, watch His ways:
> How He ruthlessly perfects whom He royally elects;
> How He hammers him and hurts him,
> And with mighty blows converts him into shapes and
>   forms of clay
> Which only God can understand,
> While man's tortured heart is crying and he lifts be-
>   seeching hands;
> Yet God bends but never breaks when man's good He
>   undertakes;
> How He uses whom He chooses,
> And with mighty power infuses him,
> With every act induces him to try His splendor out,
> God knows what he's about.

My friend, God knows what He's about—even when we don't. He knew what He was about in Mary Magdalene's life, and He knows what He's about in our lives as well. God knows what He's doing even when we don't, and He often uses disappointment to do a deeper and more detailed work.

The words of the late, great preacher and writer, A. W. Tozer, ring in my ears like a bell. He once said, "It is doubtful whether God can bless a man greatly until He has hurt him deeply." Remember the truth that deep hurts and deep disappointments design deeper and mightier disciples.

A Purpose Behind the Pain

I remember one weekend of being alone at my parents' house with my two-year-old son Jamison. It was nighttime, and on this night, I just wanted to hold him, cuddle him, and converse with him a little, but Jamison wasn't having any part of my wishes. He was too busy playing and doing what toddlers do at that age. I came up with the idea to turn out every light in the house so that it would be completely dark in every room. Guess what happened then? Jamison ran straight into my arms where I wanted him to be in the first place! My plan to allow the darkness to drive him to me worked perfectly.

Could it be that your heavenly Father has turned out the lights in your life for that very same reason? Could it be that God has orchestrated and ordained your present darkness to drive you to Him? Allow me to answer that for you. Yes!

A principle worth remembering during the dark days of disappointment is realizing that the will of God will never take you where the grace of God cannot keep you. If God's will brought dark days into your life, His grace will bring you through them. Not only was Mary Magdalene about to discover this principle for herself, she was also about to discover the truth of what King David wrote in Psalm 34:18, 19:

> *"If your heart is broken, you'll find God right there; If you're kicked in the gut, he'll help you catch your breath. Disciples so often get into trouble; still, GOD is there every time"* (MSG).

Did you catch that truth? God is there every single time—

not some, not a few, not most, but *every* time! Even during those times when you cannot see the forest for the trees or when all that could go wrong has somehow gone wrong or when you're disappointed in Him, God is there. Mary Magdalene was about to come face to face with this truth. My prayer is that you too will come face to face with this principle as well.

Point to Ponder

I am no prophet by far, but I am more than certain that some of you who are holding this book in your hands have spent your fair share of days and nights at "Disappointment Inn." Indeed, some of you are currently lodging there, and some of you likely have reservations to stay there sometime soon.

I do not make such a proclamation because I have some type of special insight. I simply know from experience and a multitude of Biblical examples that, sooner or later, life has a way of sending disappointment a person's way. Therefore, the question isn't whether or not disappointment will come; rather, the question is *when* will the disappointment come? And when that disappointment comes, how will you respond when it arrives?

For that reason, I want to pass on a piece of practical advice that will help during your time or times of disappointment. This advice revitalized my life and taught me how to deal with my disappointment in a new way. I trust what I learned will help you to handle your disappointment as well.

When disappointment comes knocking on your door, don't ask "Why?" Instead, ask "What?" "Why" questions lead to bitterness and confusion and only make matters worse. For example, don't ask:

- "*Why* did God let this happen?"
- "*Why* didn't God fix it or change it?"
- "*Why* is this person treating me this way?"
- "*Why* me? Why not someone else?"
- "*Why? Why? Why?*"

Trust me, those types of questions will only cause a person to become confused about the entire situation and bitter toward God, others, and ourselves. On the other hand, "What" questions lead to peace and joy. Some *what* questions to ask include the following:

- "*What* is God teaching me?"
- "*What* is God telling me?"
- "*What* can I learn in this situation and from this?"
- "*What* can I become from this?"

God has plenty of answers for "What" questions. *What* is a Biblical question, and therefore the person who asks "What?" has some Biblical answers as follows:

- *What* is God teaching me during my disappointments? *Patience and endurance* (James 1:3, 4), *humility* (2 Corinthians 12:7), *and obedience* (Psalm 119:67, 71).

- *What* can I become as a result of my disappointments? *Spiritually mature* (James 1:4), *a wise comforter and counselor* (2 Corinthians 1:4), *a person of greater faith* (1 Peter 1:6, 7).

- *What* can I gain from my disappointments? *Hope* (Romans 5:3-5).

The next time you are faced with a disappointment and life deals you a bad hand, don't ask "Why?" Ask "What?" Asking *what* will let you in on exactly what God is working in your life. He wants you to know, so why not ask? When we see and approach our disappointments from this standpoint, we can declare as Paul declared *"...we know that all things work together for good to those who love God, to those who are called according to His purpose"* (Romans 8:28).

"All things" include every disappointment—all my sufferings, every trial, every frustration, every storm, and every temptation. *"All"* is working together for our good! God, in His divine power and providence, is using everything that we encounter to accomplish both temporal and eternal benefits in our lives. He is using it all to shape and mold us into vessels of honor who can be used for His glory. God desires for us to become spiritually mature Christians who can endure and comfort others as He has in times past comforted us. And what God often uses is disappointment along with many other experiences to get us to that desired end.

A Prayer to Pray

God of grace and mercy, I approach You in fear and reverence. You and You alone know all, understand all, see all, and have all power. For those very reasons, I come to You with confidence and in faith.

Father, there are those who have been through the

fire and the flood. They aren't strangers to disappointment by any means. Many are strained and struggling with being disappointed right now. Many are headed in that direction. For some, disappointment has already reared its ugly head; for others, it's yet to come. But it's coming!

Whatever the case, You know how disappointment affects Your children. You know how it has the tendency to bring along with it almost unbearable pain. You also know how we are wired to ask the question "Why?" rather than "What?" Because You know us, I am asking You to deal with us according to what You know about us.

Master, meet us in our pain and show us Your purpose in the pain, but please don't stop there. Don't simply show us Your purpose in the pain but show us Your power in the pain. Keep us from becoming confused and bitter toward You, others, and ourselves.

God, lead us to the land of joy and peace, to an unspeakable joy and a peace that surpasses all understanding. In the name of Your Son, Jesus, I pray this prayer. Amen!

Part Five
Her Daylight

"You can't appreciate the miracle of the sunshine unless you've waited in the darkness."

– ANONYMOUS

CHAPTER SEVEN

WHEN MIDNIGHT TURNS TO DAYLIGHT

"Jesus said unto her, Woman, why weepest thou? Whom seekest thou?" (John 20:15, KJV).

MARY MAGDALENE'S LOYALTY and love for Jesus had caused her to linger longer at the Cross than all of Jesus' other disciples. When all the other male disciples, except for John, had fled and forsaken Jesus because of fear, Mary Magdalene stood tall and resolute as she observed the suffering of her Savior (John 19:25-27). Like refined gold, Mary Magdalene's loyalty and love for Jesus continued to shine and show up throughout her entire converted life. This same loyalty and love led Mary Magdalene back to the tomb early Sunday morning.

A Moving Observation

Joseph of Arimathea, a member of the Sanhedrin Council and a secret disciple of Jesus (John 19:38), had received permission from Pilate to retrieve the body of Christ in order to give Him a proper burial. John's gospel explains how Joseph and with Nicodemus (also a member of the Sanhedrin and a secret disciple) took the body of Jesus and bound it in strips of linen *"...with the spices, as the manner of the Jews is to bury"* (John 19:40, KJV). The entire process likely would have been done hurriedly because the Sabbath was fast approaching.

This hurried preparation of the body of Jesus by two unfamiliar faces is exactly what Mary Magdalene observed as she and the other women followed closely behind Joseph and Nicodemus. In fact, if she were even remotely familiar with these men, it would have only been through their association and affiliation with the Jewish leaders who had orchestrated the conspiracy against Jesus in the first place. All of this would have only caused Mary Magdalene and the other women who had come with her to be even more determined to prepare Jesus' body for burial themselves.

According to Luke's gospel, the women had returned home to prepare fragrant oils, and then they would have rested on the Sabbath. Their plans to wash and anoint Jesus' body properly would have taken place on the first day of the week (Luke 23:56). What Mary Magdalene observed moved her into action.

In his book, *He Still Moves Stones*, Max Lucado captures the essence of the scene I am describing ever so clearly:

> *It isn't hope* that leads Mary up the mountain to the tomb. It is duty. Naked devotion. She expects nothing in return. What could Jesus give? What could a dead man offer? Mary Magdalene is not climbing the mountain to receive; she is going to the tomb to give, period.[5]

Loyalty led her back to the tomb early Sunday morning. After considering everything that had transpired, Mary Magdalene's outlook on the whole matter was self-sacrificing. "After all Jesus has done for me, this is the least I can do for Him." Sounds a lot like the teaching of Romans 12:1 and 2, doesn't it?

> "I beseech you therefore, brethren, by the mercies of God, that you present your bodies a living sacrifice, holy, acceptable to God, which is your reasonable service. And do not be conformed to this world, but be transformed by the renewing of your mind, that you may prove what is that good and acceptable and perfect will of God."

Mary's love for Jesus led her to be a living sacrifice. In her mind, going to the tomb was part of her reasonable service. Once again displaying her loyalty and love, Mary Magdalene traveled to the tomb, planning to give Jesus the type of burial that showed someone who was deeply respected and dearly loved. However, when she arrived, things weren't as she had expected them to be.

Digesting a Dark Disappointment

Mary Magdalene arrived at Jesus' tomb early Sunday morning, the first day of the week. John felt it was worth mentioning that the day was still "dark" when she arrived (John 20:1). The day was dark because it was early in the morning, but the day was dark in another sense as well. The day was dark because of the pain from losing the One she loved was still fresh. Losing Jesus still hurt and was still hard to handle and accept. Sometimes disappointment takes a while to digest. In Mary's case, the sting of disappointment remained, and seeing a future apart from Jesus was dark and difficult for her. Sound familiar? The disappointments in our lives often cause darkness, and the darkness makes it difficult to see our future from the proper perspective.

This thought brings to the light another reason why Mary Magdalene may have gone to the tomb early Sunday morning. No doubt her primary reason for going was to properly prepare Jesus' body for burial. But perhaps she had another underlying or secondary reason. Though I cannot be dogmatic about this possibility, it is probable that Mary Magdalene went to the tomb to come to terms with the truth. She hadn't really had a chance to think through such a tragic and traumatic event. Everything had happened so fast. She now needed time to grieve. If Mary didn't enter this phase of expression, she would have entered another stage known as *suppression*, and from there most likely, depression.

A Season and a Reason to Weep

When Mary Magdalene arrived at Jesus' tomb early Sunday morning while it was still dark, to her utter surprise she discovered *"...that the stone had been taken away from the tomb"* (John 20:1). According to John, Mary Magdalene automatically assumed that someone had stolen the body of Jesus (John 20:2). As she stood outside of the tomb worried and wondering why, Mary Magdalene began to weep (John 20:11). Not only had her Savior been murdered, but now His body was missing. What else was there to do but weep? If Jesus' death was meant to knock Mary down, then surely His missing body was meant to knock her out. In Mary Magdalene's grief-stricken eyes, things had gone from bad to worse; no wonder she was weeping. Ecclesiastes 3:1, 4 says,

> *"To everything there is a season, a time for every purpose under heaven:....A time to weep and a time to laugh; A time to mourn, and a time to dance."*

The time had come for Mary Magdalene to weep. In the Greek language, the word *weep* used in John 20:11 is *klaio*, which means "to sob or wail aloud." The verb is written in an imperfect tense, which refers to a continuous or linear action in the past. This means when Mary wept outside of Jesus' tomb, it wasn't simply a few tears here and there. Mary Magdalene was weeping and wailing out loud constantly and continually. To put it in a more contemporary language, Mary Magdalene broke down! The pain was unexplainable, and the tears were unstoppable. Like water spilling from a faucet, the tears ran and kept running. Mary's season to weep had arrived.

Dr. Tony Evans, the Senior Pastor of Oak Cliff Bible Fellowship in Dallas, Texas, wrote some very informative and inspiring words concerning seasons:

> *No matter how* much you may wish to change the season you are in today, don't try to rush God's plans. If you try to change seasons on your own, you will remove yourself from God's will and lose your peace, productivity,

and power. Relish the season God has you in, and wait with patient expectation for change of seasons that will surely come.[6]

A Turning-Point Time

Mary Magdalene hadn't tried to rush or cheat her season of weeping. She had let it all out, and because she had faced and had accepted her season, she was about to see her season change before her very eyes. Mary Magdalene was about to witness a miracle. She was about to go from weeping to laughing and mourning to dancing in a matter of minutes. Thomas Fuller, the English theologian, was right when he penned the words: "It is always darkest just before the Day dawneth." Mary couldn't see it at the time, but daylight was on the horizon. The storm was disappearing, and the sunshine was reappearing. Her midnight was about to turn into daylight. The tide was about to turn!

Even as Mary Magdalene wept, two angels appeared to her, speaking directly to her: *"Woman, why are you weeping?"* (John 20:13). Though she was brokenhearted and had broken down in great grief, Mary replied anxiously through her tears, *"...Because they have taken away my Lord, and I do not know where they have laid Him"* (John 20:13).

Right then, Mary Magdalene turned and saw Jesus—though she failed to recognize Him. The Bible says she supposed *"...Him to be the gardener"* (John 20:15).

I believe this failure to recognize her Lord only confirms how much Mary Magdalene had been weeping. Her teary eyes had prevented her from recognizing Jesus. Ultimately, all Mary had been doing was weeping and imagining the worse. In reality, the worst hadn't yet happened.

Missing the Evidence

If only Mary would have considered the evidence… Indeed, considering the evidence would have been very difficult to do during times of deep pain and intense agony. However, if she had, she would have discovered the worst had not yet happened.

I have a confession to make: I am and have been a huge fan of detective shows. One of the main lessons I have learned is that in order to solve the case, you must have closely examined and followed the preponderance of evidence. If Mary Magdalene would have examined all of the evidence, she would have solved the case of Jesus' missing body. But because the pain was so profound and personal, she, like many of us, missed the obvious. Everything was there, but when your eyes are watery and your heart is weary, seeing what is in front of you can be very difficult. Don't you agree?

The truth is that Mary Magdalene missed a tremendous amount of the evidence, not purposely, but nonetheless, she missed it. She missed the evidence of the empty grave clothes (Luke 24:12; John 20:5-7). She missed the evidence of the angel's announcement: *"He is not here; for He is risen…"* (Matthew 28:6). Apparently, Mary Magdalene also missed the evidence of how excited and ecstatic Peter and John were when they left the tomb (Luke 24:12; John 20:3-8). If she would have only followed the empirical evidence, she might well have saved herself a lot of extra time and tears.

A Compassionate Call

Even though Mary Magdalene missed all the evidence of Jesus' resurrection, please don't miss the way Jesus still dealt with her in a very understanding, loving, and longsuffering way. What did Jesus do? He appeared to Mary Magdalene and asked her the same question the angel had asked with a short additive on the end: *"Woman, why are you weeping? Whom are you seeking?"* (John 20:15) And even when she didn't recognize Him because of her tear-stained eyes, what did Jesus do? He called her by name. Jesus said to her, *"Mary!"* (John 20:16).

The exclamation mark following Mary's name indicates that Jesus called her name in a manner that expressed strong passion and feeling. When Jesus called Mary's name, He called it in a distinct manner that Mary Magdalene could perceive and discern who was calling her. Jesus, in speaking about Himself, said on one occasion:

> *"...he calls His own sheep by name and leads them out. And when he brings out his own sheep, he goes before them; and the sheep follow him, for they know his voice"* (John 10:3, 4).

Jesus called Mary Magdalene by name, and once again, He led her out of darkness into the daylight. He led her out of her season of weeping into her season of laughing. He led her out of her season of mourning into her season of dancing. And she, like the loyal and loving sheep she had always been, followed Him out faithfully.

Being Known and Being Shown

Jesus' calling Mary Magdalene by name was verbal verification that He had not forgotten her. The Old Testament prophet, Isaiah, said it well in Isaiah 49:15 and 16, which says:

> *"Can a woman forget her nursing child, and not have compassion on the son of her womb? Surely they may forget, yet I will not forget you. See, I have inscribed you on the palms of My hands; your walls are continually before Me."*

Most assuredly, Jesus had not forgotten about Mary. He saw her every tear, and when He saw those tears, He was compelled to come comfort and console Mary. The same is true for you! Jesus hasn't forgotten about you. Jesus hasn't forsaken you. He has seen your every tear. He has witnessed the weeping, and those tears have compelled Him to comfort and console you—maybe not in person, but perhaps through the pages of this book. He wants to let you know that *"…weeping may endure for a night, but joy comes in the morning"* (Psalm 30:5).

In our worship service, we sing a song written by Tommy Walker entitled, "He Knows My Name." The chorus is short and simple:

> He knows my name; He knows my every thought.
> He sees each tear that falls, and hears me when I call.

Not only does He know my name and Mary Magdalene's name, the clincher is:

> He knows *your* name; He knows *your* every thought.
> He sees *your* tears that fall, and hears *you* when *you* call.

Out of Control? Under Control!

Pastor Charles (Chuck) Swindoll of the Stonebriar Community Church in Frisco, Texas, has said, "Anything under God's control is never out of control." As Mary Magdalene stood outside of Jesus' tomb weeping, her life certainly seemed to be spinning out of control. But even then, God was still in control. Confirmation is found in the fact that, after His resurrection, Jesus appeared first to Mary Magdalene (Mark 16:9). Jesus could have appeared first to anyone on earth at the time, but He chose Mary. Why? Because at that time, Mary needed Him most. She needed to be reminded of His love for her. At that time, she needed to be reminded that anything under His control is never out of control. And that includes you and your life as well. Though it may seem otherwise, nothing concerning you—your property and possessions, every person you love, and every position you hold—is out of control if it is under God's control. Nothing!

As soon as Jesus called Mary Magdalene by name, she instantly recognized who He was, and said, *"Rabboni!"* Her immediate reaction was to hug Him and cling to Him (John 20:16, 17). In the snapping of fingers, Mary had gone from hurting to happiness. Her grief and gloom were immediately replaced with unspeakable joy and delight. Only Jesus can cause such a miraculous experience. Only Jesus! This entire scenario reminds me of a few words written by the wisest man ever, Solomon:

> *"Heaviness of the heart of man maketh it stoop; but a good word maketh it glad"* (Proverbs 12:25, KJV).

> *"Hope deferred makes the heart sick, but when the desire comes, it is a tree of life"* (Proverbs 13:12).

Mary Magdalene's heart had been heavy and sick all at the same time, but one word from Jesus made her glad again. Straightaway, Mary went from stooping to standing. At once, she had gone from being miserable to being merry.

Another Resurrection

The truth is, when Mary Magdalene realized that Jesus had been resurrected, another resurrection then took place—a resurrection of Mary's faith, her trust, her peace, her joy, her smile. When Jesus died, a part of Mary died, but now that she was again standing eye to eye with the One who had liberated her by love, another resurrection took place.

She Who Is Dead Still Speaks

If Mary Magdalene could speak directly to us today, I believe she would give us some very practical advice: "When you cannot see because of the darkness and tears, don't concentrate on what you can or can't see; instead, concentrate on what God has said." More than likely, Mary would say, "Don't get caught up in the visual; get caught up in His voice. His voice wipes away every tear! His voice removes every fear!"

A Disguised Blessing

The entire time Mary Magdalene was weeping, she was weeping because she thought the worst had happened. But the truth was the worst had not happened. What Mary considered to be the worst happening was, in truth, the best thing that could ever take place wrapped in a disguise that appeared to be the worst thing. I hope you understand that because the same could be true concerning you and your situation as well. Our blessings do not always appear to be blessings until we open them up. Remember that they are often disguised until we begin to dig into them. Charles Haddon Spurgeon addressed what can be learned from times of tribulation:

> *It little matters* where we are if we can pray; but prayer is never more real and acceptable than when it rises out of the worse places. Deep places beget deep devotion. Depths of earnestness are stirred by depths of tribulation. Diamonds sparkle most amid the darkness. He who prays in the depth will not sink out of his depth. The one that cries out of the depths shall soon sing in the heights.[7]

Mary Magdalene came to Jesus' grave sobbing; she left speaking and singing *"in the heights"* (John 20:18). May the same soon be true for you. May your midnight soon turn into daylight! God is able!

A Prayer to Pray

Father in Heaven, there's no pretending with You, so we won't even try to pretend. You and You alone search the deep crevices of our hearts. You can see beyond our actions and discern our true intentions and motives, so You know the specific reason why we are praying this specific prayer at this specific hour. Therefore, we want to be as real as possible in our petitioning of You for help. We know You appreciate authenticity, and this prayer if anything, will be authentic.

Lord, there are those of us who, at this very point in time, are at the end of our rope. We have been stretched beyond our limits. We are wounded! We are weary! We are weak! We are weeping inwardly and outwardly because things have gone from bad to worse. The storm is stopping us from seeing straight. It's midnight in our lives, and that midnight hour is doing a number on us! We need Your help, Father. We are petitioning You this very hour to touch our midnight and turn it into daylight. Turn it around with Your powerful hand! Turn it around for Your glory! Don't leave us foundering in such a dark situation; penetrate it with Your power and bring light out of darkness, order out of disorder, and good out of bad.

Thank You for hearing and answering this prayer! In the name above all names—the name of Jesus—I pray. Amen.

WOMAN, WHY WEEPEST THOU?

[5]Max Lucado, *He Still Moves Stones: Everyone Needs a Miracle* (Nashville: Thomas Nelson, 2009), 41.

[6]Tony Evans and Lois Evans, *Our Love Is Here to Stay: A Daily Devotional for Couples* (Sisters, Ore.: Multnomah Publishers, 2004) March 17, 76.

[7]Charles Haddon Spurgeon, abridg. David Otis Fuller *The Treasury of David: Spurgeon's Classic Work on the Psalms* (Grand Rapids: Kregel Publications, 1976), 600.

Part Six
Our Deposit

"The tears of God's persecuted people are bottled up and sealed among God's treasures."

– MATTHEW HENRY

EPILOGUE

A MESSAGE IN A BOTTLE

"You number my wanderings; put my tears into Your bottle; are they not in Your book?" (Psalm 56:8).

YOU AND I have been on a journey following the footprints of Mary Magdalene throughout the pages of Scripture. We have keenly observed her lifestyle and life span from the salty shores of Galilee in a small village named Magdala all the way to the outskirts of Jerusalem to a place called Calvary and even beyond. Like a modern-day Sherlock Holmes, we have investigated Mary Magdalene's life thoroughly inside and out.

The Realness and Relevance of Mary Magdalene's Character

While on this journey, one of the main truths God revealed to me was the realness and relevance of Mary Magdalene's character. The gospel writers refused to paint a portrait of some type of super-saint who never missed the mark or made a mistake. On the contrary, they painted Mary Magdalene in a way that allowed us to see her both at her worse and at her best. Her character was real—not some type of fabricated fantasy drummed up in the mind of a mere man. From the sacred Scriptures, we have learned that Mary Magdalene was a real-life woman with real-life issues. For that very reason, I found myself relating to her in multiple ways. Perhaps you can make a similar statement. Perhaps you were able to relate to Mary in many ways as her life was addressed from many different angles, ranging from demonic possession and disappointment to deliverance, discipleship and devotion.

Information and Inspiration

Hopefully, what you have learned about Mary Magdalene from reading this book has not only informed you but inspired you to go above and beyond the call of duty and live a life worth living. I am trusting you have been inspired to live a life that sparkles with the gems of loyalty and love toward the One who is able to save to the uttermost and wipe away every tear. If, by reading this book, a fire has been ignited within the depths of your soul to passionately obey God, then I am well pleased and so is He. Not only that, but if you put this book down and walk away from it more assured that Jesus Christ is always anxiously awaiting to come and relieve you of every fear and every tear, then the purpose of this book has been accomplished. To God and God alone belongs the glory.

The Truth About Tears

My sincere prayer is that by reading this book you have encountered Christ and have now comprehended the magnitude of His care and compassion toward you. If His care and compassion toward Mary Magdalene compelled Him to come when she cried, then you too can rest and trust in the fact that He'll be compelled to come when you cry—every time! No matter the cause behind the cry, He's coming!

Before wrapping up this project and ending this journey, it's imperative to me that you understand the truth about tears. Your tears, my tears, Mary's tears, and many Old Testament and New Testament saints' tears are all in God's Book and His bottle. Abraham's tears are there as are Isaac's, Jacob's, Joseph's, Hagar's, Rachel's, Moses', Naomi's, Ruth's, Hannah's, and David's. So are the tears of the woman with the issue of blood and the woman caught in the very act of adultery. The tears of Lazarus' sisters, Mary and Martha, are there. Blind Bartimaeus' tears are there. The tears belonging to the man by the pool of Bethesda are there. The tears of the father whose son was having fits and seizures are there. And the list goes on infinitely.

Of course, not all of these men and women cried outwardly; some cried inwardly. Nevertheless, they cried, and their cry caught the attention of the Almighty One.

Allow me to ask you a closing question concerning tears and God's chosen people: what caused God to deliver the children of Israel from Egyptian bondage? The answer? Their tears! God said of them,

> "...I have surely seen the oppression of My people who are in Egypt, and have heard their cry because of their task masters, for I know their sorrows. So I have come

down to deliver them out of the hand of the Egyptians..." (Exodus 3:7, 8).

The children of Israel were God's chosen people; when they cried, their cry caught God's attention and provoked Him to deliver them from the oppression of their enemies.

The relevant truth is that no tear from a child of God goes unnoticed and uncollected by Him. They are securely preserved in His eternal Book and His bottle. In a very real sense, there really is a message in the bottle, and that message is, "Help, Daddy, I'm hurting!" And anytime a child of God sends that type of message to his Heavenly Daddy, He will show up and show out! He will show up and pour out His power in our situation or circumstance in ways that are unfathomable and unimaginable.

A truth worth remembering is that tears from the eyes of a child of God have always touched His heart and turned His hand. Tears are as one man meticulously described, "liquid prayers" that cause God to move mightily on the behalf of His wounded and weary children.

An Unusual Smoke Signal

In conclusion, all that has been penned before reminds me of a story. A man was stranded on a deserted island for days. He had managed to accumulate enough branches, leaves, and other materials to build a small hut. One day after going out to search for food, he came back and discovered that his little hut had burned to the ground. He was so disappointed and so

A Message in a Bottle

discouraged. Stranded without shelter, he bowed his head in anguish and began to weep. Shortly thereafter, a rescue team in a helicopter arrived and rescued the man. When he asked the rescue team how they found him, they responded by saying, "We saw your smoke signal."

I have the feeling that perhaps you can identify with the man in this story. Your "little hut" is burning right now. Right now, you're extremely familiar with the fires that can cause frustration and fear, doubt and pain. But here's the good news: the fire has set off a smoke alarm in heaven, and the God of heaven has sent a rescue team of angels to come rescue you and bring you sweet relief. Help is on the way!

You may be down right now, but you don't have to stay down nor do you have to look down. As a matter of fact, if I were you, I would begin to look up. When you look up, after a while you'll get up, and when you get up, after a while you'll go up—not just up here on earth but one day soon up to heaven. When you get there, you'll stand face to face with the One with whom Mary Magdalene stood face to face on that great Resurrection Sunday. When you stand face to face with Him beholding His splendor and glory, He will do exactly what the apostle John said He would do in Revelation 21:4:

> *"And God will wipe away every tear from your eyes; there shall be no more death, nor sorrow, nor crying. There shall be no more pain, for the former things have passed away."*

Woman, Why Weepest Thou?

Until that day, may His love for you continue to lead and liberate you repeatedly. At the same time, may your love and loyalty toward Him be continually on display in the days and weeks to come.

SCRIPTURE INDEX

CHAPTER ONE

Luke 8:2 . . . . Page 13
Isaiah 14:12-14 . . . . Page 15
Ezekiel 28:12-17 . . . . Page 15
1 Timothy 3:6 . . . . Page 15
Luke 10:8 . . . . Page 15
Revelation 12:4 . . . . Page 15
1 Corinthians 6:19, 20 . . . . Page 17
Mark 5:1-5 . . . . Page 19
Matthew 12:22 . . . . Page 19
Mark 9:17-27 . . . . Page 19
Matthew 17:15 . . . . Page 19
Luke 13:11-13 . . . . Page 19

CHAPTER TWO

Mark 16:9 . . . . Pages 25, 31
Luke 2:49 . . . . Page 25
Isaiah 61:1, 2 . . . . Pages 26, 28
Luke 4:21, 22 . . . . Page 27
Matthew 11:3-5 . . . . Pages 27, 28
Isaiah 35:5, 6 . . . . Page 28

John 8:36 . . . . Page 30
Luke 8:2 . . . . Page 31
John 15:13 . . . . Page 33
Matthew 12:43-45 . . . . Page 35
Jeremiah 13:23 . . . . Page 36

CHAPTER THREE

Luke 8:2, 3 . . . . Pages 41, 44
Proverbs 20:6 . . . . Page 42
Proverbs 31:10 . . . . Page 42
Matthew 8:16, 28, 29 . . . . Page 42
Matthew 9:32 . . . . Page 42
Matthew 12:22 . . . . Page 42
Mark 9:20 . . . . Page 43
Luke 13:12 . . . . Page 43
Mark 1:23, 24 . . . . Page 43
Luke 4:34 . . . . Page 43
Luke 8:26 . . . . Page 43
Mark 9:20 . . . . Page 43
Luke 7:36-47 . . . . Page 44
Matthew 6:21 . . . . Page 47

CHAPTER FOUR

Matthew 4:19 . . . . Page 51
Luke 6:40 . . . . Page 52
Luke 14:25-27 . . . . Pages 53, 54
Matthew 10:38 . . . . Page 53
Matthew 16:24 . . . . Page 53
Mark 8:34 . . . . Page 53

Scripture Index

Luke 9:23 . . . . Page 53
Luke 14:33 . . . . Page 54
Matthew 10:37 . . . . Page 54
Matthew 10:39 . . . . Page 55
Mark 8:35 . . . . Page 55
Luke 9:24 . . . . Page 55
Luke 17:33 . . . . Page 55
John 12:25 . . . . Page 55
Matthew 16:25 . . . . Page 55
Luke 14:28-33 . . . . Page 56
Matthew 8:18-22 . . . . Page 57
Matthew 19:16-22 . . . . Page 57
Luke 9:57-62 . . . . Pages 57, 63
Romans 8:18 . . . . Page 57
John 15:8 . . . . Page 58
Galatians 5:22, 23 . . . . Page 58
Matthew 7:16-20 . . . . Page 58
Romans 6:22 . . . . Page 58
Philippians 4:16, 17 . . . . Page 58
Hebrews 13:15 . . . . Page 58
Romans 1:13 . . . . Page 58
Romans 16:5 . . . . Page 58
Philippians 1:22 . . . . Page 58
John 15:2, 4, 5 . . . . Page 59
John 8:31 . . . . Page 60
1 John 2:19 . . . . Page 60
John 6:60-69 . . . . Pages 61, 62

CHAPTER FIVE

John 13:35	Page 65
1 John 3:18	Pages 66, 73
Matthew 22:36	Page 67
Matthew 22:37, 38	Page 67
Deuteronomy 6:5	Page 67
Matthew 22:39, 40	Page 67
Leviticus 19:18	Page 67
Romans 13:8-10	Page 68
Matthew 5:43-46	Page 69
2 Corinthians 5:14, 15	Page 70
John 13:34, 35	Page 70
1 John 3:16	Page 71
Jeremiah 31:31-34	Page 71
Ezekiel 36:24-27	Page 71
Romans 5:5	Page 71
Galatians 5:22	Page 71
Luke 24:49	Page 72
Acts 1:4-8	Page 72
1 Corinthians 13:4-8	Page 73
John 5:30	Page 74
John 6:38	Page 74
John 14:15, 21-23	Page 75
1 John 4:20, 21	Page 76
1 Peter 4:8	Page 76
Ephesians 4:15, 25	Page 77
Proverbs 27:5, 6	Page 78
Proverbs 28:23	Page 78

SCRIPTURE INDEX

CHAPTER SIX

John 19:25 .... Pages 81, 83
Psalm 119:71 .... Pages 82, 90
Matthew 27:46 .... Page 84
John 19:28 .... Page 84
John 19:30 .... Page 84
Matthew 27:55 .... Page 84
Mark 15:40 .... Page 84
Psalm 34:18, 19 .... Page 88
James 1:3, 4 .... Page 90
2 Corinthians 12:7 .... Page 90
Psalm 119:67, 71 .... Page 90
2 Corinthians 1:4 .... Page 90
1 Peter 1:6, 7 .... Page 90
Romans 5:3-5 .... Page 91
Romans 8:28 .... Page 91

CHAPTER SEVEN

John 20:15 .... Page 95
John 19:25-27 .... Page 95
John 19:38, 40 .... Pages 95, 96
Luke 23:56 .... Page 96
Romans 12:1, 2 .... Page 97
John 20:1 .... Pages 97, 98
John 20:2 .... Page 98
John 20:11 .... Page 99
Ecclesiastes 3:1, 4 .... Page 99
John 20:13, 15 .... Page 100

Luke 24:12 . . . . Page 101
John 20:5-7 . . . . Page 101
Matthew 28:6 . . . . Page 101
John 20:3-8 . . . . Page 101
John 20:15, 16 . . . . Page 102
John 10:3, 4 . . . . Page 102
Isaiah 49:15, 16 . . . . Page 103
Psalm 30:5 . . . . Page 103
Mark 16:9 . . . . Page 104
John 20:16, 17 . . . . Page 104
Proverbs 12:25 . . . . Page 105
Proverbs 13:12 . . . . Page 105
John 20:18 . . . . Page 106

EPILOGUE
Psalm 56:8 . . . . Page 111
Exodus 3:7, 8 . . . . Pages 113, 114
Revelation 21:4 . . . . Page 115

BENEDICTION
Hebrews 13:20, 21 . . . . Page 123

BENEDICTION

"Now may the God of peace who brought up our Lord Jesus from the dead, that great Shepherd of the sheep, through the blood of the everlasting covenant, make you complete in every good work to do His will, working in you what is well pleasing in His sight, through Jesus Christ, to whom be glory forever and ever. Amen."
(Hebrews 13:20, 21)